About this book

This Practice Workbook contains questions to target eve[...]sh.

Questions split into three levels of increasing difficulty – Challenge 1, Challenge 2 and Challenge 3 – to aid progress.

Symbols to highlight questions that test grammar, punctuation and spelling skills.

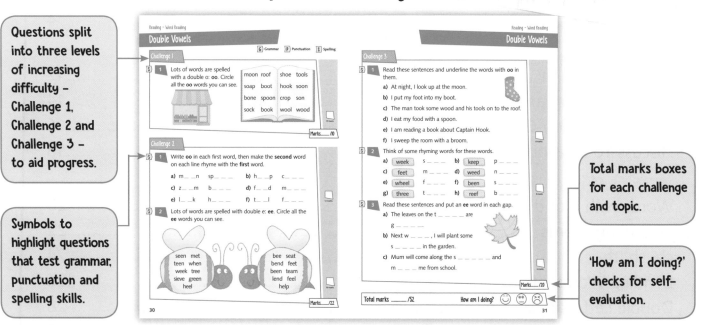

Total marks boxes for each challenge and topic.

'How am I doing?' checks for self-evaluation.

Starter test recaps skills covered in reception.

Four progress tests throughout the book, allowing children to revisit the topics and test how well they have remembered the information.

Progress charts to record results and identify which areas need further practice.

Answers for all the questions are included in a pull-out answer section at the back of the book.

Author: Jill Atkins

Contents

Contents

ACKNOWLEDGEMENTS

The author and publisher are grateful to the copyright holders for permission to use quoted materials and images.

All illustrations and images are ©Shutterstock.com and ©HarperCollinsPublishers Ltd.

Every effort has been made to trace copyright holders and obtain their permission for the use of copyright material. The author and publisher will gladly receive information enabling them to rectify any error or omission in subsequent editions. All facts are correct at time of going to press.

Published by Collins
An imprint of HarperCollinsPublishers
1 London Bridge Street
London SE1 9GF

© HarperCollinsPublishers Limited 2017
ISBN 9780008201647
First published 2017

10 9 8 7

All rights reserved. No part of this publication may be reproduced, stored in a retrieval system, or transmitted, in any form or by any means, electronic, mechanical, photocopying, recording or otherwise, without the prior permission of Collins. British Library Cataloguing in Publication Data. A CIP record of this book is available from the British Library.

Series Concept and Development: Michelle I'Anson
Commissioning Editor: Richard Toms
Series Editor: Charlotte Christensen
Author: Jill Atkins

Project Manager and Editorial: Jill Laidlaw
Cover Design: Paul Oates and Louise Forshaw
Inside Concept Design: Ian Wrigley
Text Design and Layout: Contentra Technologies
Artwork: Collins and Contentra Technologies
Production: Lyndsey Rodgers and Paul Harding
Printed in Great Britain by Bell and Bain Ltd, Glasgow

MIX
Paper from
responsible source
FSC
www.fsc.org
FSC™ C007454

This book is produced from independently certified FSC™ paper to ensure responsible forest management.

For more information visit:
www.harpercollins.co.uk/green

Starter Test

1. Practise writing this family of letters.

    a) Starting at the top of the curve, practise writing a line of the letter c.

    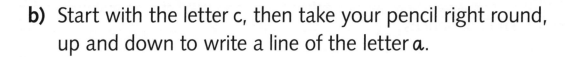

    b) Start with the letter c, then take your pencil right round, up and down to write a line of the letter **a**.

    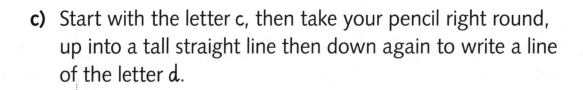

    c) Start with the letter c, then take your pencil right round, up into a tall straight line then down again to write a line of the letter **d**.

    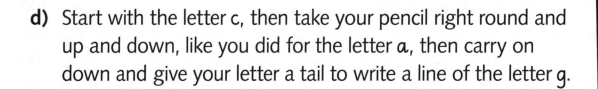

    d) Start with the letter c, then take your pencil right round and up and down, like you did for the letter **a**, then carry on down and give your letter a tail to write a line of the letter **g**.

    4 marks

2. a) Write your first name as carefully as you can.

_____

b) Now write your family name.

_____

c) Who else lives in your house? Write their names, too.

_____

_____

d) Now write the names of four friends.

_____   _____

_____   _____

8 marks

3. Words you know: **the**, **in**, **is**, **and**.

a) Write **the** in these sentences.

We went to _ _ _ park. We played on
_ _ _ swings.

b) Write **in** in these sentences.

I like to play _ _ the sand. I put sand
_ _ my bucket.

c) Write **is** in these sentences.

My dad _ _ a baker. He _ _ good at
making bread.

d) Write **and** in these sentences.

My gran _ _ _ grandad came to tea. We had
pizza _ _ _ cake.

8 marks

G Grammar   **P** Punctuation   **S** Spelling

S **4.** Look at the pictures below.

   a) Circle three pictures that begin with **s.**

   b) Write the three **s** words. _____

   _____   _____

   c) Underline three pictures that begin with **c.**

   d) Write the three **c** words. _____

   _____   _____

12 marks

S **5.** **a)** Write **a** in each gap and read the words you have made.

   c_t   h_t   t_p   m_n   b_t

   w_x   w_g   g_p   h_m   l_p

   b) Write **e** in each gap and read the words you have made.

   b_t   s_ll   n_ck   w_nt   t_ll

   l_g   b_d   p_n   b_st   s_nd

   c) Write **o** in each gap and read the words you have made.

   l_t   m_ss   t_p   l_ck   s_ng

   p_d   c_t   cl_ck   b_x   l_st

30 marks

6. Practise writing letters and numbers.

a) Copy each letter in the box.

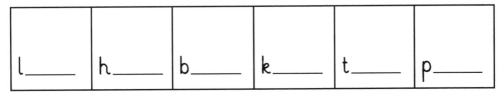

l___	h___	b___	k___	t___	p___

b) Copy each letter in the box.

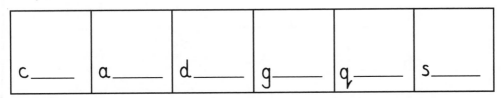

c___	a___	d___	g___	q___	s___

c) Copy each number in the box.

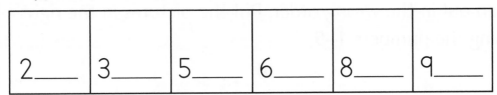

2___	3___	5___	6___	8___	9___

18 marks

7. More words that you know: **to**, **go**, **I**, **it**.

a) Write **to** in each of these sentences.

The boy ran __ __ his house. He was going __ __ watch TV.

b) Write **go** in each of these sentences.

Molly likes to __ __ to the fair. She has a __ __ on the rides.

c) Write **I** in this sentence.

If __ am a good boy, Mum says __ will get a present.

d) Write **it** in each of these sentences.

When __ __ is my birthday I will have a party. __ __ will be fun.

8 marks

S **8.** Words ending in **ck**. Write **ck** at the end of each word.

a) du _ _   li _ _   ro _ _

mu _ _   pa _ _

b) so _ _   ne _ _   Ja _ _

pi _ _   pe _ _

c) ki _ _   lu _ _   ra _ _

cli _ _   sti _ _

15 marks

9. These pictures tell the story of *The Three Little Pigs* but they have been put in the wrong order. Put the pictures in the right order using the numbers **1–5**.

a)

b)

c)

d)

e)

5 marks

10. Practise writing the alphabet in capital letters. Copy each letter on the line.

a) A   B   C   D   E

— — — — —

b) F   G   H   I   J

— — — — —

c) K   L   M   N   O

— — — — —

d) P   Q   R   S   T

— — — — —

e) U   V   W   X   Y   Z

— — — — — —

 5 marks

11. Now write the capital letter for each lowercase letter.

a ____	b ____	c ____	d ____	e ____
f ____	g ____	h ____	i ____	j ____
k ____	l ____	m ____	n ____	o ____
p ____	q ____	r ____	s ____	t ____
u ____	v ____	w ____	x ____	y ____
z ____				

 5 marks

9

GS **12.** Choose a word from the box to change each sentence.
Write the new sentence.

a)

fish	weed	bed

The <u>frog</u> swam across the pond.

_____

b)

fresh	fetch	fell

Dad went to <u>get</u> fish and chips.

_____

c)

went	will	wait

The bus had to <u>stop</u> at the traffic lights.

_____

3 marks

S **13.** Circle the words that begin with **b**.

bell
drip   big
dog dig   dart
deck   bank
   best   barn
disc boat   bulb
doll

dash
       desk
book
back   dump
        dell
bend   day
    buzz
          boss

12 marks

S **14.** Here are some more tricky words that you know: **was**, **you**, **me**, **with**.

a) Write **was** in each sentence.

The elephant _ _ _ lifting his trunk. He _ _ _ going to spray us with water.

b) Write **you** in each sentence. One '**you**' will need a capital letter.

Will _ _ _ come to the park? _ _ _ can play with a ball.

c) Write **me** in each sentence.

My mum got _ _ a doll. It has long hair like _ _.

d) Write **with** in each sentence.

I have a bike _ _ _ _ two wheels. I sometimes ride to the shops _ _ _ _ Dad.

8 marks

15. a) Write **i** in each gap. Read the words.

| d_sh | p_t | z_p | f_st | w_g |

| sk_m | f_x | b_n | ch_n | cr_sp |

b) Write **u** in each gap. Read the words.

| pl_m | c_b | s_n | j_g | t_sk |

| p_ff | m_d | b_mp | f_n | b_s |

20 marks

Listen and Join In

Ask a grown-up to read this story of *The Gingerbread Man.*

One day, an old woman made some gingerbread. She cut out the shape of a little man and popped it in the oven. After a while, she heard a high voice:

"Let me out!"

Rushing to the oven, she opened the door and out jumped the gingerbread man. He ran across the room and out of the door, calling,

"Run, run as fast as you can.

You can't catch me; I'm the gingerbread man."

The old woman ran after him.

In the garden, the gingerbread man met an old man.

"Stop!" called the old man. "You look good to eat."

But the gingerbread man laughed and called,

"Run, run as fast as you can.

You can't catch me; I'm the gingerbread man."

So the old woman and the old man ran after him.

Soon the gingerbread man met a cat.

"Stop!" meowed the cat. "You look good to eat."

But the gingerbread man shook his head and called,

"Run, run as fast as you can.

You can't catch me; I'm the gingerbread man."

So the old woman, the old man and the cat ran after him.

Soon the gingerbread man met a cow.

"Stop!" mooed the cow. "You look good to eat."

But the gingerbread man only ran faster as he called,

"Run, run as fast as you can.

You can't catch me; I'm the gingerbread man."

So the old woman, the old man, the cat and the cow ran after him.

Soon the gingerbread man reached a deep river.

He had to stop.

How was he going to get across?

At that moment, a fox crept out of the bushes.

"Jump on my tail," he barked. "I will take you across the river."

So the gingerbread man jumped onto the fox's tail and the fox began to swim.

"I'm getting wet!" he called.

"Jump on my back," barked the fox.

So the gingerbread man jumped onto the fox's back.

"I'm still getting wet!" he called.

"Jump on my nose," barked the fox.

So the gingerbread man jumped onto the fox's nose.

The fox tossed the gingerbread man in the air, opened his mouth and . . .

Snap!

That was the end of the gingerbread man!

Listen and Join In

Challenge 1

1 Join in every time you hear . . .

"Run, run as fast as you can.
You can't catch me; I'm the gingerbread man."

4 marks

Marks.......... /4

Challenge 2

1 Now answer these questions about the story. Tell your answers to the grown-up who read you the story.

a) Who made the gingerbread man?

b) Name the first animal to chase the gingerbread man.

c) Name the second animal that chased him.

d) Which animal caught the gingerbread man in the end?

4 marks

Marks.......... /4

Challenge 3

1 Here are some more questions about the story.

a) Which words in the story tell you why the old man, the cat and the cow want the gingerbread man to stop?

1 mark

b) Why did the gingerbread man have to stop?

1 mark

c) How did the fox trick the gingerbread man?

1 mark

d) Name three parts of the fox's body that the gingerbread man rode on.

3 marks

Marks.......... /6

Total marks .... /14   How am I doing?

Listen to a Story and Retell It

1 Ask a grown-up to read one of your favourite picture books to you.

Now tell the story back to the grown-up. See if you can remember what happens.

10 marks

Marks......... /10

1 Draw pictures of the story in the right order.

a) Show how it starts.

b) Draw something that happens next.

c) What happens next?

d) What happens after that?

e) How does the story end?

a)	b)

Listen to a Story and Retell It

c)

d)

e)

10 marks

Marks......... /10

Challenge 3

1

a) Talk about the story with the grown-up. Why do you like this story?

b) Talk about the characters. Are they people or animals or aliens or something else?

c) Do you like the characters? Why?

d) What are their names?

e) Which character do you like best? Why?

10 marks

Marks......... /10

Total marks .... /30   How am I doing?

Talk About a Day Out

1 Here is a picture of the seaside. Talk with a grown-up about the picture.

a) Talk about what you can see.

5 marks

b) How many children are in the picture?

_____

1 mark

c) Name four things beginning with **s**.

_____   _____

_____   _____

4 marks

d) Name two things beginning with **b**.

_____   _____

2 marks

e) What are two of the children making?

_____

1 mark

f) What are the two children in the background doing?

_____

2 marks

Marks......... /15

Talk About a Day Out

Challenge 2

1 Ask a grown-up for magazines, comics or catalogues that you can use.

a) With a friend or your brother or sister, choose some pictures of places you could go and what you could take with you. Talk about why you are choosing these pictures.

3 marks

b) Working together, see how carefully you can both cut out the pictures.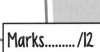

3 marks

c) Talk about how you would like to arrange the pictures and stick them on paper or in a scrapbook.

3 marks

d) When you have finished, talk about the picture you have made.

3 marks

Marks.........../12

Challenge 3

1 Talk to a friend about somewhere you have been on a day out.

a) How did you get there?

2 marks

b) Who did you go with?

2 marks

c) What did you see there?

3 marks

d) What did you enjoy most about your day out?

3 marks

e) How did you feel when you got home?

2 marks

Marks.........../12

Total marks .... /39   How am I doing?

Discuss Your Favourite Animal

1 Talk to a grown-up about your favourite animal. Is it one of the animals at the bottom of this page or a different animal?

a) Say the name of the animal.

b) Talk about why you like the animal.

c) Where does this animal live? Does it live in your house . . . or in the zoo . . . or on a farm . . . or is it a wild animal?

d) Talk about the grown-up's favourite animal.

4 marks

Marks.......... /4

Discuss Your Favourite Animal

1 What does your favourite animal look like?

a) How big is it? Say, "It's as big as . . ."

b) Talk about some animals that are bigger than your favourite animal.

c) Talk about some animals that are smaller than your favourite animal.

d) How many legs does your favourite animal have?

e) Has your favourite animal got fur, scales or smooth skin?

f) What colour is your favourite animal?

6 marks

Marks.......... /6

1 Sit with the grown-up and think about your favourite animal. Imagine it is right in front of you.

a) If you could reach out and touch it, what would it feel like? Talk with the grown-up about words you could use to describe the animal. For example, does it feel soft, warm, slippery, slimy, cold . . .?

4 marks

b) What do you think the animal would smell like?

2 marks

c) Does your animal make a noise? For example, does it roar, bark, meow, hiss . . .?

2 marks

d) How would you feel if you were right in front of this animal? For example, would you be frightened, happy, loving . . .?

2 marks

Marks......... /10

Total marks .... /20   How am I doing?

Words with b or d

G Grammar   P Punctuation   S Spelling

Challenge 1

S | **1** | Underline all the words beginning with **d**.

a) down   dress   blink   deer   bill

b) deep   brown   damp   dip   beak

c) back   bee   drink   black   doll

d) basket   dull   bank   bright   desk

10 marks

Marks......... /10

Challenge 2

S | **1** | Here are some words beginning with **d**. Write one word in each gap so the sentences make sense.

| dress | dangerous | dog | day | dark | duck |

a) A baby _____ is called a duckling.

b) Lily put on her best _____ to go to the party.

c) One _____ the little old woman made a gingerbread man.

d) William took his _____ for a walk.

e) It is very _____ to run across the road.

f) It was _____ when the lights went out.

6 marks

20

Words with b or d

S | **2** | Now here are some words beginning with **b**. Write one word in each gap so the sentences make sense.

| because | bed | blue | boy | back |

a) My favourite colour is _____.

b) My brother was cross _____ he lost his toy.

c) "Ride on my _____ ," said the fox.

d) I went to _____ and slept all night.

e) The _____ ran away from the fierce dog.

5 marks

Marks......... /11

Challenge 3

S | **1** | Look carefully at these words. Circle words that begin with **b** and end with **d**.

a) bed bark baby baked brood beep bird bend

b) bread blot bead band belt blind bold blew

10 marks

GS | **2** | Choose three of your circled words above. Write three sentences. Put one of your words in each sentence.

a) _____

b) _____

c) _____

15 marks

Marks........ /25

Total marks .... /46   How am I doing?

nk and ng Words

G Grammar   P Punctuation   S Spelling

Challenge 1

S 1 Write **nk** at the end of each word and then read each word.

a) ba___   dri___   tha___   chu___   ra___

b) thi___   su___   wi___   pla___   ho___

10 marks

Marks.........../10

Challenge 2

S 1 Now write **ng** at the end of these words and then read each word.

a) ki___   ba___   swi___   su___   cli___

b) fa___   thi___   sa___   po___   sti___

10 marks

S 2 Here are some **ng** words. Fit one into each sentence so that it makes sense.

| fang | hung | ring | long | swung |

a) The monkey _____ from branch to branch.

b) The snake got its _____ stuck in the mud.

c) The pig had a _____ in the end of its nose.

d) The bat _____ upside down in the cave.

e) The elephant has a very _____ trunk.

5 marks

Marks.........../15

22

nk and ng Words

Challenge 3

GS | **1** Here are some **ng** and **nk** words. Fit one word into each sentence so that each sentence makes sense.

| wrong | stung | drank | hang | blink | junk |

a) I was thirsty so I _____ a big glass of milk.

b) I found a load of _____ in the old shed.

c) I went the _____ way so I was lost.

d) I was _____ by a bee when I was playing in the field.

e) Mum tells me to _____ up my clothes at night.

f) I need to _____ when dust gets in my eyes.

6 marks

S | **2** Write three rhyming words for each of these words.

a) sang _____ _____ _____

b) sunk _____ _____ _____

c) song _____ _____ _____

d) sink _____ _____ _____

e) sing _____ _____ _____

f) sung _____ _____ _____

18 marks

Marks........ /24

Total marks .... /49   How am I doing?

ch, sh, th

G Grammar   P Punctuation   S Spelling

Challenge 1

S **1** Underline the words that begin with **ch**.

a) chip   cart   chap   clip

b) creep   cheep   clap   chin

c) clown   crow   chain   chop

6 marks

S **2** Circle the words that have **ch** at the end.

a) beech   pinch   leek   sink

b) arch   arm   duck   such

c) book   much   lunch   dark

6 marks

Marks.........⁄12

Challenge 2

S **1** Tick the words that begin or end with **sh**.

a) fish ☐   fill ☐   shock ☐   date ☐

b) nose ☐   mash ☐   mask ☐   shack ☐

c) dip ☐   shoot ☐   Josh ☐   job ☐

6 marks

ch, sh, th

S | **2** Underline the words that begin with **th**.

a) this   they   tree   ship   thud   tub

b) wave   that   thick   took   then   hen

6 marks

S | **3** Circle the words that end with **th**.

a) tooth   bath   bats   witch   with   such

b) bank   moth   egg   froth   dish   teeth

6 marks

Marks......... /18

Challenge 3

S | **1** Here are some words beginning with **th**.

| thin | thumb | thank | three | thief | thud |

Write one of these words in each sentence to make sense.

a) I have four fingers and one _____ on each hand.

b) I heard a loud _____ when the girl jumped off the bed.

c) I like the story of the _____ little pigs.

d) A _____ stole the big diamond.

e) The opposite of fat is _____ .

f) I _____ my friend for my present.

6 marks

Marks......... /6

Total marks .... /36   How am I doing?

Dividing Words into Syllables

Challenge 1

Some words of more than one syllable need to be split so they are easier to read. For example, rabbit can be split like this: **rab/bit**.

 1 Draw a line down each of these words to split them into syllables.

a) b u t t o n   **b)** c o f f e e   **c)** h e l m e t

d) p i c n i c   **e)** s i s t e r   **f)** f i n i s h

g) l e m o n   **h)** h a b i t   **i)** l a d d e r

9 marks

Marks.......... /9

Challenge 2

 1 Sometimes, words of two syllables are made up of two words. Split these words and write them as two separate words.

a) Sunday = _____ + _____

b) chestnut = _____ + _____

c) bedroom = _____ + _____

d) backpack = _____ + _____

4 marks

Dividing Words into Syllables

2 Add another word to each of these words to make a new word. There is a clue for each one.

a) jelly _____ (You can find them in the sea.)

b) nut _____ (A nut grows inside this.)

c) pop _____ (You might eat this at the cinema.)

d) tea _____ (You can make tea in this.)

4 marks

Marks.......... /8

Challenge 3

Some words have more than two syllables.
For example, **hip/po/pot/a/mus** has five syllables.

1 Here are some animals. Draw lines to split their names into syllables. Write how many syllables there are in each name.

a) z e b r a ☐   b) e l e p h a n t ☐

c) p a n d a ☐   d) k a n g a r o o ☐

4 marks

2 Write the two-syllable word from the clue.

a) A bird with a red breast is a _____.

b) A creature that breathes fire is a _____.

c) In a storm we have lightning and _____.

d) A baby cat is called a _____.

4 marks

Marks.......... /8

Total marks .... /25   How am I doing? ☺ ☺ ☹

27

Double Letters ff, ss, ll, zz

G Grammar   P Punctuation   S Spelling

Challenge 1

S 1 Fill the gaps in these words with **ss** and read the words.

a) | mi_ _ | fu_ _ | hi_ _ | to_ _ | pa_ _ |

b) | le_ _ | mo_ _ | dre_ _ | ki_ _ | bo_ _ |

10 marks

S 2 Fill the gaps in these words with **ll** and read the words.

a) | chi_ _ | we_ _ | du_ _ | ba_ _ | sme_ _ |

b) | se_ _ | bi_ _ | she_ _ | sha_ _ | do_ _ |

10 marks

Marks........ /20

Challenge 2

S 1 Fill the gaps in these words with **ff** and read the words.

a) (hu_ _) (sti_ _) (pu_ _) (cli_ _) (stu_ _)

b) (blu_ _) (chu_ _) (o_ _) (cu_ _) (qui_ _)

10 marks

S 2 Fill the gaps in these words with **zz** and read the words.

(bu_ _) (ja_ _) (fi_ _) (whi_ _) (fu_ _)

5 marks

Double Letters ff, ss, ll, zz

S **3** Fit one of the **zz** words from question 2 into each sentence.

a) I saw a rocket _____ up into space.

b) The bees _____ around the flowers.

c) The man played _____ on his clarinet.

3 marks

Marks......... /18

Challenge 3

S **1** Fill the gaps in these words with **ss** or **ll** and read the words.

a) | fri___ | pre___ | cre___ | thri___ | tro___ |

b) | cro___ | sti___ | che___ | spi___ | spe___ |

10 marks

S **2** Fit one of the **ss** or **ll** words from above into each sentence.

a) My dad was _____ when I spilled my milk.

b) The witch cast a _____ on her cat.

c) The _____ ran from the giant.

3 marks

S **3** Some words have a double letter in the middle.
Fit **bb** or **tt** into these words.

a) | be___er | ra___it | ki___en | ho___it |

b) | ri___on | a___ic | bo___in | bu___er |

8 marks

Marks......... /21

Total marks .... /59   How am I doing?

Double Vowels

G Grammar   P Punctuation   S Spelling

Challenge 1

S **1** Lots of words are spelled with a double o: **oo**. Circle all the **oo** words you can see.

moon	roof	shoe	tools
soap	boot	hook	soon
bone	spoon	crop	son
sock	book	wool	wood

10 marks

Marks.........../10

Challenge 2

S **1** Write **oo** in each first word, then make the **second** word on each line rhyme with the **first** word.

a) m_ _n   sp_ _ _   b) h_ _p   c_ _ _

c) z_ _m   b_ _ _   d) f_ _d   m_ _ _

e) l_ _k   h_ _ _   f) t_ _l   f_ _ _

12 marks

S **2** Lots of words are spelled with double e: **ee**. Circle all the **ee** words you can see.

seen met
teen when
week tree
sieve green
heel

bee seat
bend feet
been team
lend feel
help

10 marks

Marks........../22

Double Vowels

Challenge 3

S **1** Read these sentences and underline the words with **oo** in them.

a) At night, I look up at the moon.

b) I put my foot into my boot.

c) The man took some wood and his tools on to the roof.

d) I eat my food with a spoon.

e) I am reading a book about Captain Hook.

f) I sweep the room with a broom.

6 marks

S **2** Think of some rhyming words for these words.

a) | week | s _ _ _   b) | keep | p _ _ _

c) | feet | m _ _ _   d) | weed | n _ _ _

e) | wheel | f _ _ _   f) | been | s _ _ _

g) | three | t _ _ _   h) | reef | b _ _ _

8 marks

S **3** Read these sentences and put an **ee** word in each gap.

a) The leaves on the t _ _ _ _ are

g _ _ _ _.

b) Next w _ _ _ _ , I will plant some

s _ _ _ _ in the garden.

c) Mum will come along the s _ _ _ _ _ and

m _ _ _ me from school.

6 marks

Marks........./20

Total marks ..../52   How am I doing?

31

Real and Made-up Words

G Grammar   P Punctuation   S Spelling

Challenge 1

S 1 Circle the real words in these lists.

a) | bij | big | dat | sack | hop | hon |

b) | cag | can | cog | kit | nep | rin |

c) | tin | well | bup | buzz | feg | suv |

9 marks

Marks.......... /9

Challenge 2

S 1 Underline the made-up words in these lists.

a) | shap | ship | thit | pumt | clap | thick |

b) | malk | twop | twin | crop | moch | slam |

c) | fell | felk | drap | soon | black | bleck |

9 marks

S 2 Choose the real word to fill the gap in each sentence.

a) My dog loves to _____ at cats. **bark/birk**

b) I can play with my _____. **tays/toys**

c) When I visit my _____ she gives me cakes. **gron/gran**

d) The _____ sailed across the sea. **ship/shap**

e) I like to drink _____ at lunch time. **milt/milk**

f) I saw the _____ blowing in the wind. **flag/flug**

6 marks

Marks......... /15

Real and Made-up Words

Challenge 3

S **1** Draw lines to join beginnings and endings of words to make real words.

da

cli

fi

fo

st

mp

ld

ck

4 marks

2 Look at the letters in the flowers.

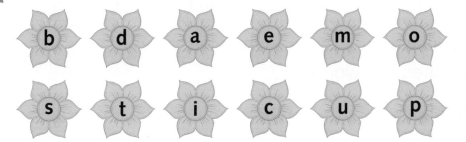

a) Make six real words from the letters in the flowers.

_____ _____ _____

_____ _____ _____

b) Now write six made-up words of your own from the letters in the flowers.

12 marks

Marks......... /16

Total marks .... /40   How am I doing?

Words You Know

Challenge 1

S | **1** Here are some words:
READ each word and try to remember how to spell it.
COVER it up.
WRITE the word in the space.
CHECK to see if you have spelled it correctly.

his	
has	
no	
so	
do	

5 marks

S | **2** Now write one of those words in each of these sentences.

a) It was cold _____ I put on my coat.

b) Sam went to feed _____ rabbit.

c) What shall we _____ when we have finished our work?

d) My friend _____ a dog.

e) Mum said there was _____ time for a story before bed.

5 marks

Marks......... /10

Challenge 2

S | **1** Here are some more words that you know.
Write them in the gaps.

once   one   house   today   ask

a) I have _____ brother and _____ sister.

b) My friend came to my _____ to play.

c) I am going to _____ for a bike for my birthday.

Words You Know

d) _____ upon a time, there lived a magic frog.

e) We are going on holiday _____.

6 marks

Marks.......... /6

Challenge 3

S | **1** Here are some words. READ each word and try to remember how to spell it. COVER it up and WRITE the word in the space then CHECK to see if you have spelled it correctly.

said	
are	
were	
come	
some	
they	

friend	
school	
where	
ask	
put	
pull	

12 marks

S | **2** Make up short sentences using the word at the beginning of each line.

a) school _____

b) friend _____

c) ask _____

d) they _____

e) said _____

5 marks

Marks......... /17

Total marks .... /33   How am I doing? ☺ 😐 😣

Answering Questions – Non-fiction

Ask a grown-up to help you read these instructions for making fairy cakes.

First, wash your hands. Then turn on the oven. Put **butter** and **sugar** in a large bowl and beat until they are light and fluffy. Whisk **eggs** in a small bowl then add them a little at a time to the butter and sugar, beating well each time. Fold in the **flour** then spoon the mixture into **cake cases**. Put them in the oven for about 20 minutes. When they are cool you can decorate them as you wish. Time to test them! Yum!

Challenge 1

1 Getting ready.

a) Write the four ingredients you need to make the cakes.

_____   _____

_____   _____

4 marks

b) What else do you need? _____

1 mark

c) What is the first thing you need to do before you start to cook?

_____

1 mark

d) What is the second thing you need to do?

_____

1 mark

Marks.........../7

36

Answering Questions – Non-fiction

Challenge 2

1 Mixing the ingredients.

a) Which two ingredients do you mix together first?

_____ and _____

2 marks

b) What do you add next? _____

1 mark

c) What do you need to do to the eggs before you mix them in?

_____

1 mark

d) Which ingredient do you add last? _____

1 mark

Marks.......... /5

Challenge 3

1 Cooking: finish off these sentences.

a) Spoon the mixture into _____ .

b) Put them in the oven for about _____ .

c) When they are cool you can _____ .

3 marks

2 Decorating the cakes. Why do you think the cakes need to be cool before you can decorate them?

_____

_____

_____

2 marks

Marks.......... /5

Total marks .... /17

How am I doing?

Answering Questions About a Story

Read this story called *Aliens in the Garden* with a grown-up.

One day, Jack was riding his bike in the garden when he heard a buzzing noise. He looked up. He saw a big round shape with red and green flashing lights.

"Wow!" he said. "A space ship!"

Down, down, down came the space ship. It landed with a thump right in front of Jack. Jack jumped off his bike, ran behind a tree and peeped.

A door in the space ship opened.

Out popped three little aliens. They had big round heads with sticking up spikes. They had long bodies with three arms and three legs.

"Ekib," said One. It jumped on Jack's bike and rode round the garden.

"Llab," said Two. It ran to Jack's ball and kicked it over the fence.

"Edils," said Three. It climbed the ladder and slid down Jack's slide.

Suddenly, Jack heard a loud 'Bleep, bleep, bleep' from the space ship. The aliens rushed back inside and took off. Jack ran into the house.

"Dad!" he shouted. "We had aliens in the garden."

Challenge 1

1   Read the story again and answer these questions.

a) What was Jack doing in the garden?

_____

1 mark

b) What kind of noise did he hear?

_____

1 mark

c) What did he see when he looked up? _____

_____

1 mark

d) Which two colours were the flashing lights?

_____   _____

2 marks

e) How many aliens were there? _____

1 mark

Marks.......... /6

Answering Questions About a Story

Challenge 2

1 Now see if you know the answers to these questions.

a) What were the aliens' heads like?

_____

b) What did the first alien do? _____

_____

c) What did the second alien do? _____

_____

d) What did the third alien do? _____

_____

4 marks

Marks.......... /4

Challenge 3

1 **a)** Write the three words the aliens said.

_____   _____   _____

3 marks

b) If you write the words backwards, what do they spell?

_____   _____   _____

3 marks

c) Do you think Jack was frightened when
the space ship landed?   _____

1 mark

d) Why do you think that?

_____

1 mark

Marks.......... /8

Total marks .... /18   How am I doing?

Reading Non-fiction

Challenge 1

1 Read this paragraph about black bears then answer the questions.

> Black bears live in forests and mountains. They are very good at climbing trees and they can run very fast. They eat grass, roots and berries as well as fish, insects, mammals and birds. They hibernate in winter. Baby bears are called cubs.

a) Where do black bears live?

_____

 1 mark

b) What are they very good at?

_____

1 mark

c) Name three things they eat.

_____ _____ _____

3 marks

d) When do they hibernate?

_____

1 mark

Marks.......... /6

Challenge 2

1 Read this paragraph about polar bears then answer these questions.

> Polar bears are white. They live on the sea ice in the Arctic and they are excellent swimmers in the icy waters. They eat mainly seals, but sometimes they eat walrus, beluga whales and birds' eggs. Newborn polar bear cubs are really small – about the size of a guinea pig!

a) What colour are polar bears? _____

1 mark

Reading Non-fiction

b) Where do they live? _____

1 mark

c) What is their main food? _____

1 mark

d) Name two more things they eat _____

_____

2 marks

e) How big are their newborn cubs? _____

_____

1 mark

Marks.......... /6

Challenge 3

Read this paragraph of fascinating facts about bears.

Bears are more afraid of humans than the other way round, but they are dangerous to humans. If bears are really hungry, they sometimes go into towns to find food. Female bears are most dangerous when they have their cubs with them. This is because they are protecting their cubs. Pandas are bears, but koalas are not!

1 Now write **true** or **false** next to these sentences.

a) Bears are more afraid of humans than the other way round. _____

b) Bears are quite cuddly so humans can go near them. _____

c) Female bears are gentle when their cubs are with them. _____

d) Pandas are not bears, but koalas are. _____

4 marks

Marks.......... /4

Total marks .... /16   How am I doing?

41

Reading Fiction

Challenge 1

1 Read this story then answer the questions.

When Ben was walking home from school he heard a loud noise. Nee-nah-nee-nah. He saw a fire engine racing towards him. It was red and silver and it had a blue flashing light on top. Ben grinned and grabbed Dad's hand. "I'm going to be a fireman when I grow up," he said.

a) What did Ben hear? _____

1 mark

b) What did he see racing towards him?

_____

1 mark

c) Name the three colours on the fire engine.

_____ _____ _____

3 marks

d) What did Ben say to his dad?

_____

1 mark

Marks.......... /6

Challenge 2

1 Read this story then answer the questions.

Mia went to the zoo with her mum and dad and her brother Tim. As they walked by the monkey house, Mia felt someone pulling her hair.
  "OW!" she shouted. "Who pulled my hair?"
  "Not me," said Tim.
  The monkey waved at Mia as if to say, "It was me!"
  Mia laughed. "Cheeky monkey!" she said.

Reading Fiction

a) Who went to the zoo with Mia?

_____ _____ _____

3 mark

b) What happened to Mia?

_____

1 mark

c) How did Mia know that it was the monkey?

_____

1 mark

d) What did Mia say? _____

1 mark

Marks.......... /6

Challenge 3

1 Read this story then put in the missing words in the sentences.

> Erin loved the seaside. As soon as she and Gran reached the beach, Erin ran towards the sea with her bucket. She collected five shells, six round pebbles and an empty crab shell. She raced back to Gran. Together, they made a giant sandcastle and decorated it with the things Erin had collected. It was just perfect!

a) Erin loved _____.

1 mark

b) She ran towards _____

with _____.

2 marks

c) She collected _____,

six round pebbles and _____.

2 marks

d) Together, they made a _____.

1 mark

Marks.......... /6

Total marks .... /18   How am I doing?

43

Poems and Rhymes

Challenge 1

1 Here is a poem. Read it more than once and see if you can learn it off by heart. Say it to a grown-up.

> There's a wide-eyed owl
> With a pointed nose,
> Feathers for fingers,
> And claws for toes.
> It looks all around and looks at you.
> It flaps its wings and says twit-twoo.

10 marks

Marks.........../10

Challenge 2

1 Answer these questions about the owl poem.

a) Which words tell us about the owl's eyes?

_____ - _____

b) What does the owl have instead of toes? _____

c) Which word rhymes with **toes**? _____

d) Which word rhymes with **you**? _____

4 marks

2 Here are some rhymes for you to finish using these words.

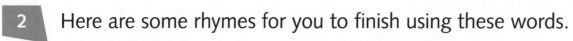

| snake | mouse | boat | box |

a) I saw a little fox sitting in a _____.

b) I heard a hissing _____. I think its name was Jake.

c) Inside an old dark house, I saw a tiny _____

d) I saw an old brown goat riding in a _____.

4 marks

Marks.........../8

Poems and Rhymes

Challenge 3

1 When we write poems we often use words that describe something. Use one of these describing words for each of these animals.

hissing	tiny	cunning	butting

a) a _____ fox **b)** a _____ snake

c) a _____ mouse **d)** a _____ goat

4 marks

2 Now get a grown-up to help you write two describing words for each of these animals.

Here are some words to choose from, but see how many more words you can think up.

tall	fierce	bouncy	snappy	friendly	cute
fluffy	scaly	wild	speedy	velvety	shy

a) dog _____

b) giraffe _____

c) crocodile _____

d) kangaroo _____

8 marks

Marks......... /12

Total marks .... /30   How am I doing?

45

1. Talk to a grown-up about the games you like to play.

   a) Are they outside or indoors?

   b) Do you play them on your own or with friends?

   c) Which do you like better: playing indoors or outside?

   d) Why?

   e) What is your favourite outdoor game?

   f) What is your favourite indoor game?

6 marks

S **2.** Write a word ending in **ff** in each sentence below.

huff	stiff	off	puff	cliff

   a) We sat on the beach at the bottom of the _ _ _ _ _.

   b) Amy jumped _ _ _ the board into the pool.

   c) The card was so _ _ _ _ _ I could not bend it.

   d) Will the wolf _ _ _ _ and _ _ _ _ and blow the house down?

5 marks

S **3.** Add **ch** to each of these words.

a) (mun _ _) (fin _ _) (mu _ _) (bea _ _)

(_ _ eese)

b) (_ _ ill) (su _ _) (_ _ ick) (_ _ air)

(_ _ eep)

10 marks

S **4.** Draw a line to split each word into two syllables.

a) b a m b o o   b) h o b b i t   c) w a g o n

d) t o p i c   e) c a r r o t   f) b u t t e r

g) f i f t e e n   h) c a n d y   i) p o c k e t

9 marks

5. Write a two-syllable word in each of these sentences.

| backpack | kitten | dentist | zebra | ladder |

a) A _____ is an animal with black and white
stripes.

b) When I go to school I carry
my _____ on my back.

c) A baby cat is called a _____.

d) The man climbed a _____ to clean
the windows.

e) The _____ looks after my teeth.

5 marks

6. Read this passage and write **true** or **false** after each sentence below.

> Elephants are the largest land animals in the world. Some elephants live for 70 years. Elephants cannot see well, but they have a very strong sense of smell through their long trunks. They also use their trunks for lifting heavy things, for putting food and water in their mouths and for spraying water over themselves. They live in family groups and look after their calves very well.

a) Elephants see well. _____

b) Elephants live by themselves. _____

c) Some elephants live for 70 years. _____

d) Elephants leave their calves after they are born.

_____

e) Elephants are the largest land animals in the world.

_____

f) Elephants' trunks are very useful. _____

6 marks

7. Write a rhyming word for each of these animals:

a) fox _____   **b)** cat _____

c) dog _____   **d)** pig _____

e) mouse _____   **f)** goat _____

6 marks

S **8.** Here are some words spelled with an **oo** or **ee** sound. Write one word in each sentence so that it makes sense.

| school cheese boot shoot been pool feel queen |

a) I have _____ to London to visit the

_____.

b) My sister and I _____ down the chute at the

swimming _____.

c) I have a _____ sandwich for my lunch

at _____.

d) When I put on my _____ I _____ a
hard stone.

8 marks

9. Words that you know. Write one of the words below in each sentence so it makes sense.

(**to**) (**and**) (**you**) (**was**)

a) Mum said I _____ a very good girl at the shops.

b) I will give _____ a lovely present.

c) We are going _____ see my favourite film today.

d) For my party food we will have fish _____ chips.

4 marks

Marks........./59

49

Word Endings

G Grammar P Punctuation S Spelling

Challenge 1

S **1** If a word ends with a **v** sound, it usually ends **ve**. Write **ve** on the end of these words and read them out loud.

a) ca __ __   b) fi __ __   c) car __ __   d) li __ __

e) ha __ __   f) sha __ __   g) arri __ __   h) lo __ __

i) sa __ __   j) hi __ __

10 marks

S **2** Write one of these words in each sentence.

drive   twelve   beehive   dive

a) Bees make honey in a _____ .

b) I can _____ into the swimming pool.

c) My mum can _____ a big truck.

d) I have _____ friends coming to my party.

4 marks

Marks......... /14

Challenge 2

S **1** Join each pair of rhyming words with a line.

glove   sleeve

wave   give

arrive   love

leave   dive

live   gave

5 marks

50

Word Endings

S **2** Add **tch** to the end of each of these words and read them aloud.

a) ba _ _ _   **b)** pi _ _ _   **c)** wa _ _ _

d) hu _ _ _   **e)** wi _ _ _   **f)** la _ _ _

g) no _ _ _   **h)** fe _ _ _   **i)** ha _ _ _

9 marks

Marks......... /14

Challenge 3

S **1** The letter **y** at the end of words can sound like **i** or like **ee**. Read these words aloud. Listen to the **y** at the end.

> try   very   fly   spy   merry   fairy   cry   fry
>
> happy   why   shy   puppy   silly   by   windy   mummy

a) Circle the words that rhyme with **my**.

b) Underline the words where the **y** sound is the same as the **y** in **party**.

16 marks

S **2** Choose from the words ending in **y** above to fill the gaps in these sentences.

a) It was _____ so we went out to _____ a kite.

b) The _____ clown made us laugh.

c) My _____ takes me to school every day.

3 marks

Marks......... /19

Total marks .... /47   How am I doing?   😊   😐   😣

Different Spellings for Sounds

G Grammar   P Punctuation   S Spelling

Challenge 1

S 1 **igh**, **ie**, **i_e** and **y** can sound the same. Here are some **igh**, **ie**, **y**, **i_e** words.

a) Circle the words with **igh** in them.

b) Write the four words with **i_e** in them.

_____ _____

_____ _____

light
tight   by
lie   tie   fight
side   might   try
bite   like   fright
kite   sight
cry
sigh
fly
my

7 marks

4 marks

Marks.......... /11

Challenge 2

S 1 Write a word from the kite above in each sentence.

a) The loud noise gave me a _ _ _ _ _ _ _.

b) _ _ sister upset me and made me _ _ _.

c) I can _ _ _ _ _ _ shoelaces.

d) A button popped off because my coat was too

_ _ _ _ _.

e) I _ _ _ _ _ to play in the park.

f) I use my teeth to _ _ _ _ _ my food.

8 marks

S 2 Now write three more words you know with **i_e** in them.

_____ _____ _____

3 marks

52

Different Spellings for Sounds

S **3** **oi** and **oy** sound the same, but **oy** usually comes at the end of a word (boy) and **oi** is in the middle of a word (noise).

Write two words that rhyme with each of these words:

a) toy _____ _____

b) boil _____ _____

c) loin _____ _____

6 marks

Marks......... /17

Challenge 3

S **1** Write an **oi** or **oy** word in the gaps in these sentences.

a) I found my lost tractor in the t __ __ box.

b) I am a __ __ __ and my sister is a girl.

c) I tossed a c __ __ __ into the fountain and made a wish.

3 marks

S **2** **ai**, **ay** and **a_e** sound the same.

a) Tick the boxes of all the **ai** words and underline the **a_e** words.

train	☐	take	☐	chain	☐
name	☐	brain	☐	shade	☐

b) Write three **ay** words that rhyme with **play**.

_____ _____ _____

9 marks

Marks......... /12

Total marks .... /40   How am I doing? 😊 😐 😖

Days of the Week

G Grammar   P Punctuation   S Spelling

Challenge 1

S 1 Copy the days of the week in your best handwriting. Start each one with a capital letter.

Sunday _____

Monday _____

Tuesday _____

Wednesday _____

Thursday _____

Friday _____

Saturday _____

7 marks

S 2 Answer these questions.

a) How many days are there in a week? ☐

1 mark

b) Which two days are the weekend days?

_____ and _____

2 marks

Marks......... /10

Challenge 2

S 1 a) Write the one day that has seven letters. _____

1 mark

b) Write three days with six letters. _____

_____   _____

3 marks

c) Write the one day that has nine letters.

_____

1 mark

Marks......... /5

Days of the Week

Challenge 3

 1 Finish these sentences with something you might do. It doesn't have to be true!

a) On Sunday, I _____

b) On Monday, I _____

c) On Tuesday, I _____

d) On Wednesday, I _____

e) On Thursday, I _____

f) On Friday, I _____

g) On Saturday, I _____

 7 marks

 2 Cover the rest of these two pages and test yourself. See if you can write the days of the week without peeking.

a) S _____

b) M _____

c) T _____

d) W _____

e) T _____

f) F _____

g) S _____

 7 marks

Marks......... /14

Total marks .... /29   How am I doing?

Adding er and est

Challenge 1

When we write about things or people we use words to describe them.

For example, 'a **smart** person'.

If we add **er** to **smart** it shows that a person is more smart than somebody else (a **smarter** person).

1   Write these words then add **er** to each of them.

a) long _____   b) small _____

c) cheap _____   d) clean _____

e) kind _____

5 marks

S   **2**   Look at the picture and write **taller** or **shorter** in the gaps.

a) Alex is _ _ _ _ _ _ than Sam.

b) Sam is _ _ _ _ _ _ _ than Alex.

Alex   Sam

2 marks

Marks.......... /7

Challenge 2

If we add **est** to the word **smart** it shows a person is the most smart of everybody (the **smartest** person).

S   **1**   Write these words then add **est** to each of them.

a) strong _____   b) mean _____

c) thick _____   d) light _____

e) dark _____

5 marks

Adding er and est

2 Fill the gaps in these sentences with the **est** words below.

greenest   darkest   cheapest

a) The horse wanted to eat the _ _ _ _ _ _ _ _ grass.

b) My mum bought the _ _ _ _ _ _ _ _ pair of shoes in the shop.

c) At night, the sky is the _ _ _ _ _ _ _ shade of blue.

3 marks

Marks......... /8

Challenge 3

1 Write these words then add **er** and **est** to them.

a) cold _____   _____

b) loud _____   _____

c) quick _____   _____

6 marks

2 Use these words to fill the gaps in these sentences.

a) The fridge is _ _ _ _ _ _ than the kitchen,

but the freezer is the _ _ _ _ _ _ _ _.

b) I can shout _ _ _ _ _ _ than you, but my

brother is the _ _ _ _ _ _ _ _.

c) When we raced, Helen was _ _ _ _ _ _ _ than

Tom, but I was the _ _ _ _ _ _ _ _.

6 marks

Marks......... /12

Total marks .... /27   How am I doing? 😊 😐 😣

57

er, ir, ur; oa, o_e

G Grammar   **P** Punctuation   **S** Spelling

Challenge 1

S **1** **er**, **ir** and **ur** can sound the same. Read these words and underline the **er** words.

a) fern   girl   turn   kerb   verb

b) bird   term   burn   her   perch

c) hurt   herd   germ   dirt   hers

9 marks

S **2** Write an **er** word in each gap in these sentences.

(term) (kerb) (her) (herd) (verb)

a) The little girl played with _ _ _ doll.

b) We start a new _ _ _ _ after the holidays.

c) There is a _ _ _ _ of cows in the field.

d) A _ _ _ _ is a doing or being word.

e) I stand on the _ _ _ _ and look both ways before I cross the road.

5 marks

Marks......... /14

Challenge 2

S **1** Write three words with **ir**.

_____   _____   _____

3 marks

S **2** Write three words with **ur**.

_____   _____   _____

3 marks

S **3** Write an **ir** word in each gap in these sentences.

| stir | dirty | bird | girl |

a) I got my hands _ _ _ _ _ in the garden.

b) The _ _ _ _ was sitting on its nest.

c) I saw a _ _ _ _ running away from me.

d) I _ _ _ _ _ some milk into my tea.

4 marks

Marks......... /10

Challenge 3

S **1** **o_e** and **oa** can sound the same.

Here are some **o_e** and **oa** words. Underline the **o_e** words and circle the **oa** words.

a) bone   boat   soap   toast   joke

b) load   robe   nose   toad   doze

c) croak   zone   road   rope   loaf

15 marks

S **2** Use some of the words in question 1 above to fill the gaps in these sentences.

a) I use _ _ _ _ to wash my hands.

b) I heard a _ _ _ _ _   _ _ _ _ _ down by the pond.

c) Dad cuts the _ _ _ _ of bread to make

some _ _ _ _ _ _.

d) The clown had a red _ _ _ _ _. He told a funny

_ _ _ _.

7 marks

Marks........ /22

Total marks .... /46   How am I doing?   ☺ 😐 😣

59

ow and ou

G Grammar   P Punctuation   S Spelling

Challenge 1

> **ow** has two different sounds. The first sound is like the **ow** in bl**ow**.

S 1 The **ow** sounds the same in the words below. Write one **ow** word in each sentence.

snow	slow	grow	flow	below

a) I was too _ _ _ _ so I missed the bus.

b) When I _ _ _ _ up I will be an athlete.

c) I hid _ _ _ _ _ the bridge so no one could find me.

d) I watched the river _ _ _ _ past me.

e) The field was covered in white _ _ _ _.

5 marks

Marks.......... /5

Challenge 2

> The second **ow** sound is like the ow in **cow**.
>
> These words have **ow** at the end.
>
> | how | now | cow | wow |
> |-----|-----|-----|-----|
>
> These **ow** words have **ow** inside them or at the beginning.
>
> | clown | owl | down | shower | brown | gown |
> |-------|-----|------|--------|-------|------|

S 1 Write one **ow** word that rhymes with these words. (Don't use any of the examples given above.)

a) clown _____   b) owl _____

c) shower _____

3 marks

Marks.......... /3

ow and ou

Challenge 3

ou sounds the same as the **ow** in c**ow**. Here are some examples.

round   mouth   proud   stout

S **1** Write a rhyming **ou** word for each of these words.

a) round _____   **b)** mouth _____

c) proud _____   **d)** stout _____

4 marks

S **2** Write the **ow** words inside the cow.
Write the **ou** words inside the mouth.

crown	town	around	hound	proud
shower	clown	mouth	about	loud
flower	cow	pout	found	frown	round

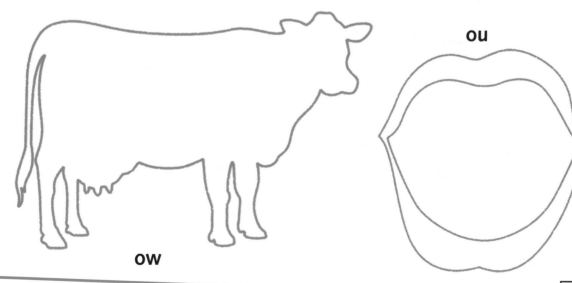

ou

ow

16 marks

Marks........ /20

Total marks .... /28   How am I doing?

ph, wh and k

G Grammar   **P** Punctuation   **S** Spelling

Challenge 1

S **1** **ph** is sometimes used for the **f** sound. Underline the words with **ph** in them.

phonics   alphabet   finger   face   phone

3 marks

S **2** Circle the animals spelled with **ph**.

ferret   frog   elephant   fox   dolphin

2 marks

S **3** Tick the names that have **ph** in them.

Fujika ☐   Rudolph ☐   Sophie ☐

Freddy ☐   Phuong ☐

3 marks

Marks.......... /8

Challenge 2

S **1** Use **ph** words from Challenge 1 to fill each gap.

a) I saw an _ _ _ _ _ _ _ _ at the zoo.

b) I like to sing _ _ _ _ _ _ _ _ the Red-nosed Reindeer.

c) I know all the letters of the _ _ _ _ _ _ _ _ _.

d) The _ _ _ _ _ _ _ _ swims quickly and jumps out of the water.

4 marks

S **2** Some words beginning with the **w** sound are spelled **wh**. Write a word in each gap.

white   whisper   wheel   whiskers   whistle

a) The _ _ _ _ _ cat had long _ _ _ _ _ _ _ _.

b) The old cart has lost a _ _ _ _ _.

c) I heard a _ _ _ _ _ _ _ then a quiet _ _ _ _ _ _ _.

5 marks

ph, wh and k

S | **3** These **wh** words are often used to ask questions. Fill in the gaps to make questions.

| When | Where | Which | Why | What |

a) _ _ _ _ can you come to my house to play?

b) _ _ _ did you run away?

c) _ _ _ _ _ would you like for tea?

d) _ _ _ _ _ _ cake would you like?

e) _ _ _ _ _ _ shall we go tomorrow?

5 marks

Marks......... /14

Challenge 3

S | **1** Sometimes we use **k** instead of **c** for the **k** sound. Fit these **k** words into the gaps.

| kettle | koala | kangaroo | kitten |

a) A baby _ _ _ _ _ _ _ _ _ is called a joey.

b) Dad boiled the _ _ _ _ _ _ to make a cup of tea.

c) A _ _ _ _ _ _ is a baby cat.

d) A _ _ _ _ _ is an Australian animal.

4 marks

2 Write a rhyming word beginning with **k** for each of these words.

a) sing _____   b) white _____

c) bit _____   d) hid _____

4 marks

Marks......... /8

Total marks .... /30   How am I doing? ☺ ☹ 😣

ar, or and air

Challenge 1

S **1** Here are some words with **ar** in them. Draw a line between the words that rhyme.

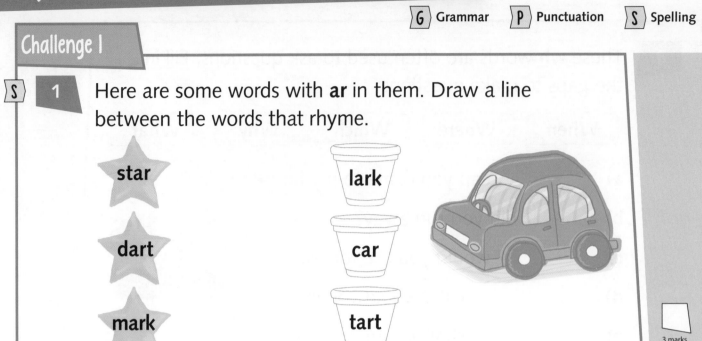

star

dart

mark

lark

car

tart

3 marks

Marks.........../3

Challenge 2

S **1** Answer the clues and write the **ar** words in this crossword puzzle.

| bark | start | smart | shark |

a) 2 Across: Very clean and neat

b) 3 Across: A very fierce fish

c) 1 Down: The noise a dog makes

d) 2 Down: Begin

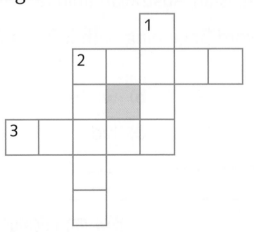

4 marks

ar, or and air

 2 Here are some words with **or** in them.

fork	storm	port	horn	porch	cord
corn	form	ford	cork	torch	fort

Choose one of the **or** words for each sentence.

a) I eat my dinner with a knife and _ _ _ _.

b) I switched on my _ _ _ _ _ when the lights went out.

c) The boy blew loudly on his toy _ _ _ _.

d) The ship sailed into _ _ _ _.

4 marks

Marks.......... /8

Challenge 3

 1 Write the words from the box in Challenge 2 question 2 in rhyming pairs.

Example: fork   cork

a) _____   _____

b) _____   _____

c) _____   _____

d) _____   _____

e) _____   _____

10 marks

Marks.......... /10

Total marks .... /21   How am I doing?

Consonant Blends

Challenge 1

Consonant blends are when two or three consonants are together in a word and the consonants make their own sound. For example, two consonants **bl** and **gr**; three consonants **spl** and **spr**.

S **1** Circle the words with a consonant blend at the beginning.

a) grit   deep   frog   drip   clap

b) stop   skin   bean   seep   flat

c) beat   swim   scab   keel   plan

10 marks

S **2** Join these rhyming words with a line.

drab	twin
stop	drip
slip	slap
skin	crab
clap	plop

5 marks

Marks......... /15

Challenge 2

S **1** Underline the words with a consonant blend at the end.

a) lost   desk   bean   bank   meal

b) zeal   left   land   gate   junk

c) wasp   foot   lift   gulp   risk

10 marks

Consonant Blends

2 Write words that rhyme with each of these words.

a) best   r_____

b) camp   l_____

c) loft   s_____

d) must   j_____

e) melt   b_____

f) pump   b_____

g) land   h_____

h) bent   w_____

8 marks

Marks.......... /18

Challenge 3

1 Tick the words with a consonant blend at the beginning and at the end.

a) track ☐   **b)** twin ☐

c) twist ☐   **d)** crank ☐

e) peal ☐   **f)** crisp ☐

g) trunk ☐   **h)** down ☐

i) fair ☐   **j)** stamp ☐

6 marks

2 Write a short sentence using these words:

a) twist _____

b) trunk _____

c) crisp _____

d) stamp _____

4 marks

Marks.......... /10

Total marks .... /43   How am I doing?   ☺   😐   ☹

Progress Test 2

S **1.** **a)** Write three **ai** words that rhyme with **main**.

_____   _____   _____

b) Write three **a_e** words that rhyme with **same**.

_____   _____   _____

c) Write three **ay** words that rhyme with **bray**.

_____   _____   _____

9 marks

S **2.** Write the days of the week that you go to school.

_____   _____

_____   _____

_____   _____

5 marks

S **3.** Here are some describing words. Add **er** to each of them and fit them into these sentences.

light	long	grand	loud	quick

a) A palace is _ _ _ _ _ _ _ than a house.

b) A feather is _ _ _ _ _ _ _ _ than a stone.

c) A snake is _ _ _ _ _ _ than a worm.

d) A cheetah is _ _ _ _ _ _ _ _ than an elephant.

e) A trumpet is _ _ _ _ _ _ than a whisper.

5 marks

68

S **4.** Put these **y** words into two lists.

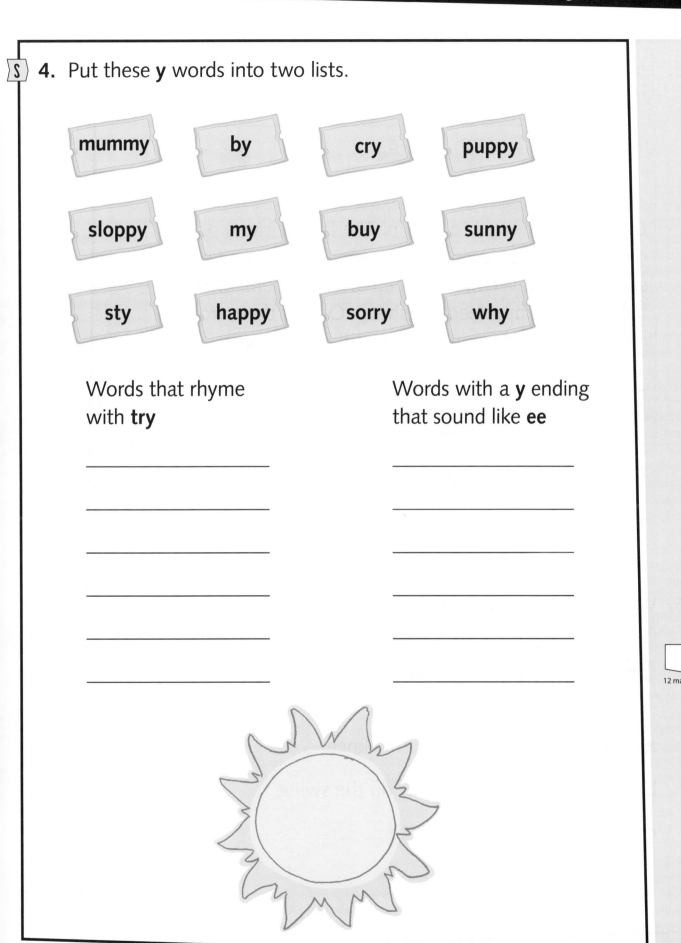

mummy by cry puppy

sloppy my buy sunny

sty happy sorry why

Words that rhyme
with **try**

Words with a **y** ending
that sound like **ee**

_____   _____

_____   _____

_____   _____

_____   _____

_____   _____

_____   _____

12 marks

G Grammar P Punctuation S Spelling

S **5.** How many different **ee** words can you find in this passage? Write them on the lines below.

Last week, we went to a farm. The farmer came out to meet us. He took us in his jeep across the green fields to see the sheep. We had to creep towards them. Then we helped the farmer feed the sheep. One of them trod on my feet! I fell asleep in the car on the way home.

_____   _____   _____

_____   _____   _____

_____   _____   _____

_____

10 marks

S **6.** Write these **ur** words in the sentences.

burn   hurt   turn

a) I fell over and _ _ _ _ my knee.

b) It is my _ _ _ _ to play on the swing.

c) Dad put a log on the fire to _ _ _ _ _.

3 marks

S **7.** Fill in the crossword by answering these clues with **ch** words.

a) 3 Across: It is made from milk

b) 4 Across: You can travel in this

c) 5 Across: Part of the face on either side of the nose

d) 6 Across: Underneath your mouth

e) 1 Down: Another name for a hen

f) 2 Down: I love you so _____!

6 marks

S **8.** Use each clue to write a two-syllable word.

a) A baby dog is called a _ _ _ _ _.

b) The place where we sleep is called a _ _ _ _ _ _ _ _.

c) If we take our food out to the park we have a _ _ _ _ _ _ _.

d) The number after fifteen is _ _ _ _ _ _ _ _.

e) The man climbed a _ _ _ _ _ _ _ to get up to the roof.

5 marks

Marks........./55

Writing Stories: Beginning, Middle and End

Challenge 1

1 Here is the beginning of a story. Read it then answer the questions.

> Once upon a time, there lived a boy called Prince Harry.
> One day, he saw a red and yellow kite high in the sky.
> "I wish I had a kite like that," he said.
> He ran to his mother, Queen Lily.
> "Mum," he said. "Will you buy me a red and yellow kite?"

a) Write the four words that sometimes begin a traditional

story. _____

1 mark

b) Write your own idea for what happened next. _____

_____

_____

3 marks

Marks.......... /4

Challenge 2

1 Now read on. Here is the middle part of the story.

> The queen smiled, but shook her head.
> "Fetch me a tail feather from the brightest peacock in the gardens," she said. "Then I will buy you a kite."
> So Prince Harry ran into the garden and found the brightest peacock.
> "Please will you give me one of your tail feathers?" he asked the peacock. "It is for my mother, Queen Lily. Then she will buy me a kite."

Writing Stories: Beginning, Middle and End

a) Do you think the peacock said yes? _____

b) Write your own idea for what happened next. _____

_____

_____

Marks.......... /4

Challenge 3

1 Now read on. Here is the end of the story.

> The peacock held his head up high.
> "I am the king of the birds," he squawked.
> "So I need a crown. Give me your crown
> and I will give you one of my tail feathers."
> So Prince Harry took off his crown and
> gave it to the peacock.
> The peacock pulled out a tail feather
> and gave it to Prince Harry.
> Prince Harry ran back to Queen Lily and gave her
> the feather.
> "Thank you," she said and she gave Prince Harry a
> red and yellow kite.

a) Do you think Prince Harry should have
given the peacock his crown? _____

b) What would you have done?

_____

Marks.......... /2

Total marks .... /10   How am I doing?

Planning a Story

For these questions, continue your answers on a separate piece of paper if you need to.

Challenge 1

1 Talk to a grown-up about making up your own story about aliens.

   a) Write what it will be about. _____

   _____

   _____

   _____

4 marks

   b) Where will this story happen? _____

   _____

1 mark

2 Think about who will be in your story. Write some alien names:

   a) The main character _____

   b) Two other characters _____ and _____

2 marks

3 Is your main character good, funny or scary? _____

1 mark

Marks.........../8

Challenge 2

1 Make a storyboard. Write words or sentences and draw pictures to show what will happen to your characters. Let them have a really exciting adventure.

1	2	3

Planning a Story

4	5	6

12 marks

2 Talk about how your story begins. What will your first sentence be? Write it down.

2 marks

Marks......... /14

Challenge 3

1 Use your storyboard to remember what comes next. Talk about it then write it down.

2 marks

2 Talk about the exciting things that happen next and write them here.

5 marks

3 Make up a good ending and write it down.

2 marks

Marks......... /9

Total marks .... /31   How am I doing?   😊 😐 😣

In the Right Order

Challenge 1

1 Here is a very short story, but it has been jumbled up.
Put the sentences in the right order by numbering them
1, 2 and 3.

a) Five chicks hatched out of the eggs. ☐

b) A bird made a nest. ☐

c) Then the bird laid five eggs. ☐

3 marks

2 Write one sentence about what might happen next.

_____

_____

1 mark

Marks.......... /4

Challenge 2

1 Here are some instructions for making a sandwich.
Put them in the right order by numbering them
1, 2, 3, 4 and 5.

a) Put the cheese on one slice of bread. ☐

b) Spread the bread with butter. ☐

c) Put the second slice of bread on top of the first one. ☐

d) Take two slices of bread. ☐

e) Cut slices of cheese. ☐

5 marks

2 Write one sentence about what might happen next.

_____

_____

1 mark

Marks.......... /6

In the Right Order

Challenge 3

1 Here are some sentences about a day out at the beach, but they are jumbled up in the wrong order. Put them in the right order by numbering them 1, 2, 3, 4, 5 and 6.

a) It was time to go home so we went back to the car. ☐

b) After that, we had our picnic lunch. ☐

c) In the afternoon, we swam in the sea. ☐

d) We got to the seaside at 10 o'clock. ☐

e) Then we ran to the sea to wash off the sand. ☐

f) The first thing we did was make a big sandcastle. ☐

6 marks

2 Write the sentences here in the right order and read the story you have written.

1 _____

2 _____

3 _____

4 _____

5 _____

6 _____

6 marks

Marks.........../12

Total marks ..../22

How am I doing?

Giving Instructions

1 Pretend that an alien has come to visit you. Tell the alien how you clean your teeth.

a) What do you do first?

_____

b) What do you do next?

_____

c) Write what else you do. _____

_____

d) Draw a really strange alien cleaning its teeth.

4 marks

Marks.......... /4

1 Tell the alien about what you do as you get up in the morning and get ready for school.

1 First, I _____

2 Then, I _____

3 Next, I _____

4 Then, I _____

5 After that, I _____

5 marks

Giving Instructions

2 What do you think an alien would do if it went to school with you?

_____

_____

2 marks

Marks.......... /7

Challenge 3

1 Imagine you are the alien! Tell your friend how you came down to Earth in a flying saucer. Write as carefully as you can.

1	
2	
3	
4	
5	
6	
7	

10 marks

Marks......... /10

Total marks .... /21   How am I doing?

79

Writing Letters

For any of the questions below, continue your answer on a separate piece of paper if needed.

Challenge 1

1 It will soon be your birthday and you are going to have a party. Write a letter inviting your friend to the party.

a) Begin with 'Dear.......' (write your friend's name).

b) Write the day of the party, the time of the party (.......o'clock) and where the party will be held.

c) End the letter with 'Love from.......' (write your name).

_____

_____

_____

_____

3 marks

Marks.........../3

Challenge 2

1 You have had a happy birthday with lots of presents. Your uncle Tim sent you some money to buy something you would like. Write a thank-you letter to uncle Tim.

a) Begin 'Dear Uncle Tim'.

b) Thank him for the money.

c) Tell him what you might buy.

d) End the letter.

Writing Letters

_____

_____

_____

_____

4 marks

Marks.......... /4

1   Your nan and grandad sent you a new bicycle. You are so excited. You wish you could thank them face-to-face, but they live a long way away. So write them a letter.

a) Begin 'Dear Nan and Grandad'.

b) Thank them for the bike and tell them about riding it.

c) Tell them about your party.

d) End the letter.

_____

_____

_____

_____

_____

7 marks

Marks.......... /7

Total marks .... /14   How am I doing?   😊   😐   😣

Writing about Real Experiences

Challenge 1

1 Do you like watching TV? What is your favourite TV programme? Talk about it with a grown-up, then write about it in the box below.

2 marks

2 Answer these questions about your favourite programme.

a) Why do you like it? _____

b) What is your favourite part? _____

c) Who is your favourite character? _____

3 marks

Marks.......... /5

Challenge 2

1 Do you like going to the park? Does it have a playground with things to climb on? Is there a pond? Can you see birds or animals there? Write about a visit to the park. Say who you went to the park with and what you did.

_____

_____

_____

_____

_____

5 marks

Writing about Real Experiences

2 What was the best thing you did on your visit to the park?

_____

1 mark

Marks.......... /6

Challenge 3

1 Talk about an outing you have been on. It could be with your teacher and your class or with family or friends. Remember where you went and what you did there. Write as much as you can about it.

_____

_____

_____

_____

_____

5 marks

2 Answer these questions.

a) Did you enjoy the outing? _____

b) What was the most enjoyable part? _____

c) How did you feel when you got home? _____

_____

3 marks

Marks.......... /8

Total marks .... /19   How am I doing?

G Grammar **P** Punctuation **S** Spelling

1. Read this passage then answer the questions with **true** or **false**.

> Snakes are reptiles. Their bodies are covered in scales and they shed their skin as they grow. They live on land and in water. Some snakes are poisonous. Most snakes eat small animals like frogs, insects and birds, but the biggest snakes can eat large animals like deer – whole!

a) Snakes are mammals. _____

b) Snakes' bodies are covered in fur. _____

c) Snakes live on land and in water. _____

d) All snakes are poisonous. _____

e) Snakes shed their skin. _____

f) The biggest snakes can eat large animals whole. _____

6 marks

S 2. Here are words that you know. Write one word in each sentence so it makes sense.

are	said	where	they

a) My grandad _ _ _ _ he was coming to dinner.

b) I do not know _ _ _ _ _ I left my coat.

c) My friends told me _ _ _ _ would meet me at school.

d) How _ _ _ you?

4 marks

3. Here are some describing words. Ask a grown-up to help you choose one for each gap in these sentences.

> greedy   fantastic   bright   lumpy   sparkling   brave

a) The _____ boy ate all the cakes.

b) The lights were _____ and _____ on the tree.

c) Henry was rescued by a _____ person.

d) I have a _____ collection of cars.

e) I have a _____ pillow on my bed.

6 marks

GS **4.** Add **er** and **est** to each word to make it **more** and **the most**.

a) short _____ _____

b) bright _____ _____

c) slow _____ _____

6 marks

S **5.** Circle the words that rhyme with **batch**.

much	catch
match	thatch
bash	cash
lunch	witch
latch	such
patch	hatch

6 marks

[S] **6.** Use the clues to fill in the crossword with **ph** words.

   a) 4 Across: An animal with a trunk

   b) 5 Across: A girl's name

   c) 1 Down: A sea mammal

   d) 2 Down: The letters and sounds that you learn

   e) 3 Down: All the letters of the a_____

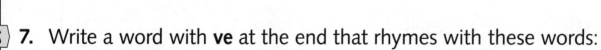

5 marks

[S] **7.** Write a word with **ve** at the end that rhymes with these words:

   a) shave _____

   b) glove _____

2 marks

8. Read this passage with an adult then answer the questions.

> The clown looked very funny. He had white make-up on his face, black crosses on his eyes and a big red nose. He wore baggy green and red trousers and a floppy yellow hat.

a) What colour was the make-up on the clown's face?

_____

1 mark

b) What did he have on his eyes? _____

1 mark

c) What colour was his nose? _____

1 mark

d) Which two words describe his hat?

_____ and _____

2 marks

e) Which two colours were the clown's trousers?

_____ and _____

2 marks

f) Which other word describes his trousers? _____

1 mark

g) Draw a clown to match him. Colour your picture in.

2 marks

Marks........ /45

Singular and Plural

Challenge 1

GS | **1** Copy the plural of the singular words in the box next to each one. The first one has been done for you.

dog	dogs
book	
brick	
ant	
cup	

tin	
ship	
light	
peg	
rug	

9 marks

Marks.......... /9

Challenge 2

GS | **1** Add **es** to each of these singular words to make them plural. The first one has been done for you.

dish	dishes
fizz	
peach	
boss	
hutch	
six	

arch	
bus	
dress	
ditch	
fox	
smash	

11 marks

Marks.......... /11

Singular and Plural

Challenge 3

GS **1** Add either **s** or **es** to these singular words to make them plural.

buzz	
elephant	
melon	
witch	
hill	
crash	

kiss	
banana	
box	
gas	
name	
tax	

12 marks

GS **2** Fill the gap in each sentence with one of these words.

| bananas names bricks boxes |

a) The third little pig's house was made of _____.

b) The monkey ate six _____ and threw the skins on the ground.

c) At home, I have three _____ full of toys.

d) The children stood in a row and told me their

_____.

4 marks

Marks........ /16

Total marks .... /36   How am I doing?

Spaces and Sentences

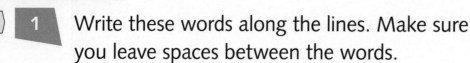

G) Grammar   P) Punctuation   S) Spelling

P) 1 Write these words along the lines. Make sure you leave spaces between the words.

a) fish   and   chips

_____

b) brother   and   sister

_____

c) in   the   park

_____

3 marks

Marks.........../3

P) 1 Now write these words along the lines, making sure you use finger spaces. There are extra words to make them into a sentence.

a) i   like   fish   and   chips

_____

_____

b) i   have   a   brother   and   a   sister

_____

_____

c) we   had   fun   in   the   park

_____

_____

3 marks

Marks.........../3

Spaces and Sentences

Challenge 3

P **1** We need to use punctuation in writing. All sentences begin with a capital letter and some end with a full stop. Write out the same sentences you wrote in Challenge 2, putting in the capital letter and full stop.

a) _____

_____

b) _____

_____

c) _____

_____

3 marks

P **2** Write out these sentences, using a capital letter at the beginning of each one and a full stop at the end.

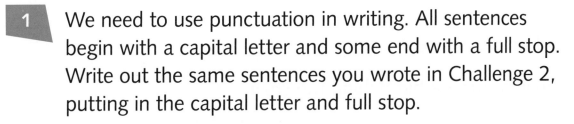

a) the rocket zoomed up into space

_____

b) the dog ran across the grass

_____

c) it was so dark we had to switch on the lights

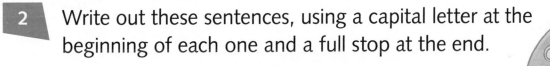

_____

d) there were three monkeys in the zoo

_____

4 marks

Marks.......... /7

Total marks .... /13

How am I doing?

91

Capital Letters and Full Stops

G Grammar **P** Punctuation **S** Spelling

P | **1** Draw a circle round where the capital letter and full stop should be in each sentence.

a) the little mouse hid behind the chair

b) the crocodile has very sharp teeth

c) the teddy has a big bow

d) the clown has a big red nose

e) the clock struck nine

10 marks

Marks........./10

P | **1** Write each sentence correctly by adding a capital letter and a full stop.

a) i like to eat an apple for lunch

_____

b) i wear gloves when the weather is cold

_____

c) the baby was smiling at me

_____

Capital Letters and Full Stops

d) the plane landed at the airport

_____

e) the elephant has white tusks

_____

10 marks

Marks......... /10

Challenge 3

P **1** There are two sentences in each box below, but they need to have capital letters and full stops. Add them in the right places.

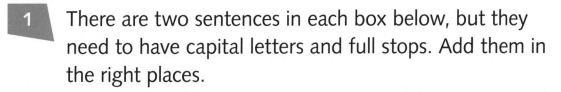

Example: the baby was smiling at me. i waved to her and she waved back.

a) i like to eat an apple for lunch apples are sweet and juicy

b) the dog ran across the grass it ran after a cat

c) the elephant has white tusks they are quite long

d) the plane landed at the airport the people had been on holiday

8 marks

Marks......... /8

Total marks .... /28

How am I doing?

Capital Letters

G Grammar   P Punctuation   S Spelling

Part of using the right punctuation is about using capital letters in the right place.

When you are writing about yourself, you need to use a capital **I**.

P | **1** Correct these sentences by neatly crossing out the lowercase letter and writing in the capital letter for all the words that need it.

a) in winter, i put on my gloves so i can go outside.

b) i love going to the fair because i love the rides.

c) my brother is taller than me because i am much younger.

d) i think a cat is the best animal and i love to hear it purr.

9 marks

Marks.......... /9

Another punctuation rule is to use a capital for names as well as for Mr and Mrs. For example,

My friend **M**ia has a teacher called **M**r **P**inch.

P | **1** Write these sentences. Use capital letters in the right places.

a) i invited rose, sandeep, erin and david to my party.

_____

_____

b) my sister esha said i was silly.

_____

c) yash and grace played with the cars, but i played by

myself. _____

_____

d) narinda and i went up and down on the seesaw.

_____

e) my teacher is called mrs west and i like her.

_____

f) i think i will beat amy in the race because i can run fast.

21 marks

_____

Marks.........../21

Challenge 3

P **1** You also need to use capital letters for towns
and countries. Underline all the letters that
should be capitals in these sentences.

a) yesterday i went to london.

b) paris is the capital of france.

c) sami and i went to brighton, which is by the sea.

d) we went to spain on holiday and i went to the beach.

11 marks

Marks.........../11

Total marks ..../41   How am I doing?

Question Marks

G Grammar   P Punctuation   S Spelling

Challenge 1

P **1** When you write a question you need to put a question mark at the end of the sentence. Add a question mark to the end of each sentence. Make sure you write your question mark correctly, like this ?

a) Where are you going__

b) Why do you want to come to the fair__

c) Do you like pizza or salad best__

d) When will you get a pet__

e) What is your favourite animal__

5 marks

P **2** Add the question marks and then answer the questions with **yes** or **no**.

a) Do you like horses__   _____

b) Would you like to ride a horse__ _____

2 marks

Marks.......... /7

Challenge 2

P **1** Add the question marks then answer the questions.

a) What is a baby dog called__ _____

b) What is a baby cat called__ _____

c) What is a baby sheep called__ _____

d) What is a baby pig called__ _____

e) What is a baby fox called__ _____

f) What is a baby chicken called__ _____

6 marks

Question Marks

P | **2** Add a question mark or full stop at the end of the sentences.

a) My dad reads to me at bedtime ___

b) Does your mum have long hair ___

c) When will you come and play with me ___

d) The baby is very happy ___

4 marks

Marks......... /10

Challenge 3

P | **1** Use a question mark at the end of each of these sentences.

a) Write any question you might ask your mum or dad.

_____

1 mark

b) Write any question you might ask your teacher.

_____

1 mark

c) Write any question you might ask your friend. Write it in the first speech bubble then write an answer in the second bubble.

2 marks

Marks......... /4

Total marks .... /21

How am I doing?

97

Exclamation Marks and Other Punctuation

G Grammar   P Punctuation   S Spelling

Challenge 1

P **1** Add an exclamation mark to each of the following:

a) Look out __

b) How exciting __

c) What a lucky girl you are __

d) That is a lovely big parcel __

e) Wow __

5 marks

Marks.......... /5

Challenge 2

P **1** Add capital letters and exclamation marks to these:

a) i cannot believe it

b) you have grown such a lot since april

c) be quiet

d) what a lot of books you have read

e) how fantastic

5 marks

P **2** Some of these sentences need exclamation marks, some need full stops and some need capital letters. Punctuate the sentences.

a) mum and i went to the shops

b) the hat she bought was fabulous

c) it was amazing

d) we came home and showed Dad

e) dad said it was fantastic

5 marks

Marks........ /10

Exclamation Marks and Other Punctuation

Challenge 3

P **1** Imagine you are talking to a friend. Add capital letters, full stops, exclamation marks and question marks to these sentences.

a) we went to the zoo on saturday

b) what did you see there

c) we saw an elephant

d) was it big

e) it was enormous

5 marks

P **2** Here is another little story of two people talking. Put in the capital letters and the correct punctuation.

a) i have been out with my gran

b) where did you go

c) she took me to see a film

d) did you have a good time

4 marks

3 Make up your own answer to part **d)** above that needs an exclamation mark. Write your answer in the speech bubble.

1 mark

Marks.........../10

Total marks ..../25

How am I doing?

99

Using and to Join Words and Clauses

G Grammar   **P** Punctuation   **S** Spelling

Challenge 1

G **1** Write **and** in the gaps to make a pair that go together.

a) fish _____ chips

b) shoes _____ socks

c) bucket _____ spade

d) horse _____ cart

e) cup _____ saucer

f) knife _____ fork

g) bacon _____ eggs

h) left _____ right

i) king _____ queen

j) boys _____ girls

10 marks

Marks......... /10

Challenge 2

G **1** Write **and** after each word then add the opposite of that word.

Example: high __and__ __low__

a) dark _____ _____

b) hard _____ _____

c) big _____ _____

d) happy _____ _____

e) heavy _____ _____

f) empty _____ _____

g) hot _____ _____

h) fast _____ _____

8 marks

G **2** Join these short sentences with **and**.

a) I am a boy _____ my name is Jack.

b) I can run fast _____ I win all the races.

c) I love reading _____ I have lots of books.

Using and to Join Words and Clauses

d) I have a cat _____ her name is Tabby.

e) I play with Ling _____ she is my best friend.

5 marks

Marks......... /13

Challenge 3

6

1 Add **and**, then finish with your own ending.

a) I went to the farm _____.

b) My nan came to my house _____.

c) I played football _____.

d) I have a wiggly tooth _____.

4 marks

2 Copy out these sentences, adding the word **and** where it should go.

Example: The weekend days are Saturday <u>and</u> Sunday.

a) My brother is called Ethan my sister is called Emily.

_____

_____

b) I like apples bananas, but my favourite fruits are strawberries cherries.

_____

_____

2 marks

Marks.......... /6

Total marks .... /29

How am I doing?

Prefix un

 G Grammar  **P** Punctuation **S** Spelling

Challenge 1

S **1** Write **un** in front of each of these words to make them mean the opposite.

a) ____happy **b)** ____do

c) ____fit **d)** ____lucky

e) ____pack

 5 marks

Marks.......... /5

Challenge 2

S **1** Write the opposite of these words by adding **un** at the beginning.

a) tie _____ **b)** dress _____

c) tidy _____ **d)** even _____

e) true _____

 5 marks

2 Here are some words beginning with **un**. Write one of them against each meaning.

unload unplug unhook untrue untidy

a) take off a hook _____

b) messy _____

c) false _____

d) pull plug out _____

e) remove a load _____

 5 marks

Marks........ /10

Prefix un

Challenge 3

S **1** Choose the correct spelling of the **un** word to fill the gaps in these sentences.

a)

unlode	unloud	unload

I helped Dad _____ the dishwasher.

b)

undone	undon	undun

Your buttons are _____ .

c)

unzipp	unzep	unzip

Help me _____ my coat.

d)

unloc	unlock	unlok

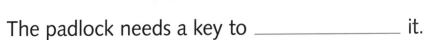

The padlock needs a key to _____ it.

e)

unwell	unwil	unwel

I am feeling a bit _____ .

5 marks

S **2** Write a word beginning with **un** that means the same as each of these words.

a) sad _____

b) ill _____

c) take clothes off _____

d) in danger _____

4 marks

Marks.......... /9

Total marks .... /24

How am I doing?

Adding ing, ed or er

Challenge 1

S **1** Here are some doing or being words. Doing or being words are called verbs.

| help | jump | kick | climb | open | follow |

Add **ing** to each of the words and read the new words out loud.

a) help_____   b) jump_____

c) follow_____   d) climb_____

e) open_____   f) kick_____

6 marks

Marks.........../6

Challenge 2

S **1** Add **ed** to the words.

a) help_____   b) jump_____

c) follow_____   d) climb_____

e) open_____   f) kick_____

6 marks

Adding ing, ed or er

S **2** Choose one of these **ed** words to fit in these sentences.

climbed	jumped	opened

a) Mum _____ the window to let the fresh air in.

b) I _____ a mountain when we were on holiday.

c) I _____ up and down on the trampoline.

3 marks

Marks........... /9

Challenge 3

1 Add **er** to the words.

a) help_____   **b)** jump_____

c) follow_____   **d)** climb_____

e) open_____   **f)** kick_____

6 marks

S **2** Choose from the words below and add **ing**, **ed** or **er** to fill the gaps in each sentence. The first letter of each word has been given for you.

help	jump	kick	climb	open	follow

a) The dog f_ _ _ _ _ _ _ _ the man all the way home.

b) I love being a h_ _ _ _ _ _ in the classroom.

c) A sheep looks like it is wearing a woolly j_ _ _ _ _ _ !

d) Dad was o_ _ _ _ _ _ _ a tin of dog food with a

tin o_ _ _ _ _ _.

5 marks

Marks........... /11

Total marks .... /26   How am I doing?

Correcting Your Work

G Grammar   **P** Punctuation   **S** Spelling

Challenge 1

G **1** Think about an adventure story involving a boy and a girl. Talk to a grown-up about your story.

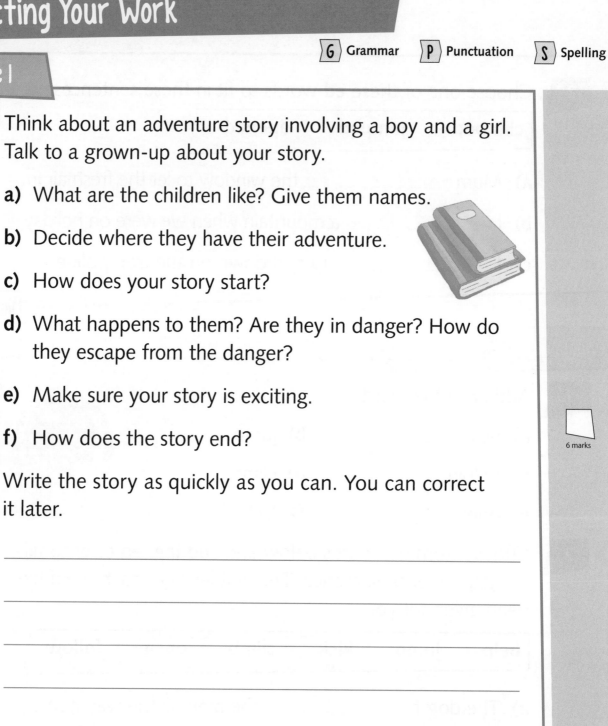

  a) What are the children like? Give them names.

  b) Decide where they have their adventure.

  c) How does your story start?

  d) What happens to them? Are they in danger? How do they escape from the danger?

  e) Make sure your story is exciting.

  f) How does the story end?

6 marks

2 Write the story as quickly as you can. You can correct it later.

_____

_____

_____

_____

_____

_____

_____

10 marks

Marks......... /16

Correcting Your Work

Challenge 2

S | 1 | Read the story you have written. Check all the spellings and correct them if you need to.

5 marks

GS | 2 | Have you got capital letters, full stops, question marks and exclamation marks in the right places? Correct them if you need to.

5 marks

Marks......... /10

Challenge 3

GPS | 1 | Now write your story out again in your best handwriting. Make sure the spelling and punctuation are correct.

_____

_____

_____

_____

_____

_____

_____

10 marks

2 | Check your story again and read it out loud.

5 marks

Marks......... /15

Total marks .... /41   How am I doing? ☺ 😐 😖

Progress Test 4

P **1.** Rewrite these sentences, putting capital letters in the right places.

   a) jack and mia went to london.

   _____

   b) i have a best friend called pippa.

   _____

   c) i go to school on monday, tuesday, wednesday, thursday and friday.

   _____

3 marks

P **2.** Write a word beginning with **sh** that rhymes with these words.

   a) chip _____

   b) bell _____

   c) hop _____

   d) but _____

   e) crack _____

5 marks

SG **3.** Add **s** or **es** to these singular words to make them plural.

   a) bus_ _   **b)** watch_ _   **c)** leg_

   d) stair_   **e)** patch_ _   **f)** boy_

   g) laptop_   **h)** hiss_ _   **i)** flash_ _

9 marks

4. Write these sentences in the right order to make a well-known story. Remember to use full stops and capital letters.

a) Then she went to her grandmother's house.

b) First, she picked some flowers in the woods.

c) A woodcutter rescued Little Red Riding Hood.

d) Little Red Riding Hood waved goodbye to her mum.

e) A wolf was in her grandmother's bed.

f) The wolf had eaten Little Red Riding Hood's grandmother.

_____

_____

_____

_____

_____

_____

12 marks

5. Write these words beginning with **wh** in the gaps so the sentences make sense.

what	where	which	when	why

a) _____ would you like to go to the beach?

b) _____ teddy bear would you like?

c) _____ are you crying?

d) _____ is the time?

e) _____ did you put my pencil?

5 marks

S) 6. Write two words that have **ou** or **ow** spellings that rhyme with each of these words:

    a) cloud   _____   _____

    b) down   _____   _____

    c) now   _____   _____

    d) bound   _____   _____

    8 marks

S) 7. READ each word and try to remember how to spell it.
COVER it up.
WRITE the word in the space.
CHECK to see if you have spelled it right.

    a) | come | _____

    b) | some | _____

    c) | put | _____

    d) | pull | _____

    8 marks

SG) 8. For each sentence below, choose one of the words from question 7 to complete the sentence.

    a) I always _____ my toys away when I have finished playing.

    b) Will you _____ to my house for tea?

    c) I tried to _____ open the door but it was locked.

    d) I have _____ pencils in a box.

    4 marks

P **9.** Write a full stop, question mark or exclamation mark at the end of each sentence.

a) What a noise they are making＿

b) Would you like a slice of melon＿

c) I love seeing spring flowers in the woods＿

d) The ostrich is a very large bird, but it cannot fly＿

e) How marvellous you look＿

f) How old are you＿

6 marks

S **10.** Choose one of these word endings to add to the letters below to make a real word.

| mp | lk | sp | nd |

a) mi ＿ ＿   b) cri ＿ ＿   c) chi ＿ ＿

d) be ＿ ＿   e) plu ＿ ＿   f) da ＿ ＿

g) fu ＿ ＿   h) si ＿ ＿

8 marks

P **11.** Fit these words ending in **nk** into each sentence.

bunk   sank   junk   tank

a) The fish were swimming in a glass ＿＿＿＿＿＿＿＿.

b) The stone ＿＿＿＿＿＿＿＿ to the bottom of the pond.

c) I love to sleep on the top ＿＿＿＿＿＿＿＿.

d) Mum says my bedroom is full of ＿＿＿＿＿＿＿＿.

4 marks

Marks.........../68

111

Notes

Pages 4–11 Starter Test

1. a) A neatly written line of 'c'.
   b) A neatly written line of 'a'.
   c) A neatly written line of 'd'.
   d) A neatly written line of 'g'. **(4 marks)**

2. a) Child to write her/his first name.
   b) Child to write her/his family name.
   c) Child to write names of whoever lives in their home.
   d) Child to write the names of four friends. **(8 marks)**

3. a) We went to <u>the</u> park. We played on <u>the</u> swings.
   b) I like to play <u>in</u> the sand. I put sand <u>in</u> my bucket.
   c) My dad <u>is</u> a baker. He <u>is</u> good at making bread.
   d) My gran <u>and</u> grandad came to tea. We had pizza <u>and</u> cake. **(8 marks)**

4. a) Circled: star, sun, snake
   b) The **s** words: star, sun, snake, all spelled correctly.
   c) Underlined: cup, cake, cat
   d) The **c** words: cup, cake, cat, all spelled correctly. **(12 marks)**

5. a) cat, hat, tap, man, bat
      wax, wag, gap, ham, lap
   b) bet, sell, neck, went, tell
      leg, bed, pen, best, send
   c) lot, moss, top, lock, song
      pod, cot, clock, box, lost **(30 marks)**

6. a) Neatly written l, h, b, k, t, p
   b) Neatly written c, a, d, g, q, s
   c) Neatly written 2, 3, 5, 6, 8, 9 **(18 marks)**

7. a) The boy ran <u>to</u> his house. He was going <u>to</u> watch TV.
   b) Molly likes to <u>go</u> to the fair. She has a <u>go</u> on the rides.
   c) If <u>I</u> am a good boy, Mum says <u>I</u> will get a present.
   d) When <u>it</u> is my birthday I will have a party. <u>It</u> will be fun. **(8 marks)**

8. a) duck, lick, rock, muck, pack
   b) sock, neck, Jack, pick, peck
   c) kick, luck, rack, click, stick **(15 marks)**

9. 1. c)   2. b)
   3. e)   4. d)
   5. a) **(5 marks)**

10. a)–e) Correct formation of capital letters. **(5 marks)**

11. Correct formation of capital letters, 1 mark for each correct row, final row to include 'z'. **(5 marks)**

12. a) The <u>fish</u> swam across the pond.
    b) Dad went to <u>fetch</u> fish and chips.
    c) The bus had to <u>wait</u> at the traffic lights. **(3 marks)**

13. bell, big, bank, barn, bend, bulb, best, boat, book, back, buzz, boss **(12 marks)**

14. a) The elephant <u>was</u> lifting his trunk. He <u>was</u> going to spray us with water.
    b) Will <u>you</u> come to the park? <u>You</u> can play with a ball.
    c) My mum got <u>me</u> a doll. It has long hair like <u>me</u>.
    d) I have a bike <u>with</u> two wheels. I sometimes ride to the shops <u>with</u> Dad. **(8 marks)**

15. a) dish, pit, zip, fist, wig
       skim, fix, bin, chin, crisp
    b) plum, cub, sun, jug, tusk
       puff, mud, bump, fun, bus **(20 marks)**

Pages 12–13
Challenge 1
1. Award marks for joining in the refrain. **(4 marks)**
Challenge 2
1. a) the old woman   b) the cat
   c) the cow   d) the fox **(4 marks)**
Challenge 3
1. a) "You look good to eat." **(1 mark)**
   b) he came to a river **(1 mark)**
   c) he said he would help the gingerbread man across the river **(1 mark)**
   d) tail, back, nose **(3 marks)**

Pages 14–15
Challenge 1
1. Award marks for remembering the story well with a lot of details. Award fewer marks for a less detailed account. **(10 marks)**
Challenge 2
1. Award 2 marks for each picture a)–e) as long as each picture is drawn in the true sequence of events of the story. Award fewer marks if the order is incorrect or if there is not much detail. **(10 marks)**
Challenge 3
1. Award 2 marks for each question, a)–e), provided there is some detail as required, e.g. d) names of characters. **(10 marks)**

Answers

Pages 16–17
Challenge 1
1. a) Award marks for detailed observation and
        discussion of the picture. **(5 marks)**
    b) five **(1 mark)**
    c) **Any four from:** sand, sea, starfish, spade or
        any other s words noticed.
        (4 marks)
    d) **Any two from:** bucket, bus, ball, boy or
        any other b words noticed. **(2 marks)**
    e) sandcastles **(1 mark)**
    f) playing with a ball and doing cartwheels/
        handstands **(2 marks)**

Challenge 2
1. a) Award marks for detailed conversation
        with the child, e.g. discussion of what the
        pictures are of and why the pictures were
        chosen. **(3 marks)**
    b) Award marks for conversation while
        cutting. **(3 marks)**
    c) Award marks for conversation about
        picture arrangement: discussion,
        negotiation, agreement. **(3 marks)**
    d) Award marks for discussion, e.g. whether
        child is happy with what s/he has
        achieved, what the pictures show.
        (3 marks)

Challenge 3
1. a) Award marks for how much detail is given
        about the journey. **(2 marks)**
    b) Award marks for detail about the people
        s/he went with. **(2 marks)**
    c) Award marks for information given about
        what was seen. **(3 marks)**
    d) Award marks for expression of enjoyment
        and detail of that. **(3 marks)**
    e) Award marks for expression of feeling,
        language used. **(2 marks)**

Pages 18–19
Challenge 1
1. a) name of animal given by child
    b) reason given by child
    c) where the animal lives
    d) discussion of grown-up's favourite animal
        (4 marks)

Challenge 2
1. a) Award mark for simile "as big as....."
    b) encourage child to give information about
        bigger animals
    c) encourage child to give information about
        smaller animals

d) encourage child to give information about
    how many legs
e) encourage child to give information about
    the animal's skin type
f) encourage child to give information about
    the animal's colour(s) **(6 marks)**

Challenge 3
1. a) Award marks for words used to describe
        the animal; 4 marks for four words;
        3 marks for three words; 2 marks for two
        words; 1 mark for one word. **(4 marks)**
    b) Award marks for language used to
        describe smell. **(2 marks)**
    c) Award marks for sounds the animal might
        make. **(2 marks)**
    d) Award marks for words used to show how
        the child might feel. **(2 marks)**

Pages 20–21
Challenge 1
1. a) down, dress, deer **b)** deep, damp, dip
    c) drink, doll **d)** dull, desk
        (10 marks)

Challenge 2
1. a) A baby <u>duck</u> is called a duckling.
    b) Lily put on her best <u>dress</u> to go to the
        party.
    c) One <u>day</u> the little old woman made a
        gingerbread man.
    d) William took his <u>dog</u> for a walk.
    e) It is very <u>dangerous</u> to run across the
        road.
    f) It was <u>dark</u> when the lights went out.
        (6 marks)
2. a) My favourite colour is <u>blue</u>.
    b) My brother was cross <u>because</u> he lost his
        toy.
    c) "Ride on my <u>back</u>," said the fox.
    d) I went to <u>bed</u> and slept all night.
    e) The <u>boy</u> ran away from the fierce dog.
        (5 marks)

Challenge 3
1. a) bed, baked, brood, bird, bend
    b) bread, bead, band, blind, bold **(10 marks)**
2. a), b) and c) award up to 5 marks for each
        sentence: each sentence must include a
        chosen word beginning with **b** and ending
        with **d**; each sentence must be a full sentence;
        each sentence must make sense; check for
        punctuation; award the final marks for interest
        or description. **(15 marks)**

Pages 22–23
Challenge 1
1. a) bank, drink, thank, chunk, rank
    b) think, sunk, wink, plank, honk   **(10 marks)**
Challenge 2
1. a) king, bang, swing, sung, cling
    b) fang, thing, sang, pong, sting   **(10 marks)**
2. a) The monkey <u>swung</u> from branch to branch.
    b) The snake got its <u>fang</u> stuck in the mud.
    c) The pig had a <u>ring</u> in the end of its nose.
    d) The bat <u>hung</u> upside down in the cave.
    e) The elephant has a very <u>long</u> trunk.
                                              (5 marks)

Challenge 3
1. a) I was thirsty so I <u>drank</u> a big glass of milk.
    b) I found a load of <u>junk</u> in the old shed.
    c) I went the <u>wrong</u> way so I was lost.
    d) I was <u>stung</u> by a bee when I was playing in the field.
    e) Mum tells me to <u>hang</u> up my clothes at night.
    f) I need to <u>blink</u> when dust gets in my eyes.   **(6 marks)**
2. a) **Any three from:** bang, clang, fang, gang, hang, pang, rang, twang or other suitable answer.
    b) **Any three from:** bunk, clunk, chunk, dunk, drunk, gunk, hunk, junk, slunk, stunk or other suitable answer.
    c) **Any three from:** bong, dong, gong, long, pong, wrong or other suitable answer.
    d) **Any three from:** clink, chink, drink, link, mink, rink, kink, sink, slink, stink, think, wink or other suitable answer.
    e) **Any three from:** cling, ding, fling, king, ping, ring, sting, sling or other suitable answer.
    f) **Any three from:** clung, dung, flung, hung, lung, rung, stung, slung, young or other suitable answer.   **(18 marks)**

Pages 24–25
Challenge 1
1. a) chip, chap   b) cheep, chin
    c) chain, chop   **(6 marks)**
2. a) beech, pinch   b) arch, such
    c) much, lunch   **(6 marks)**
Challenge 2
1. a) fish, shock   b) mash, shack
    c) shoot, Josh   **(6 marks)**
2. a) this, they, thud
    b) that, thick, then   **(6 marks)**

3. a) tooth, bath, with
    b) moth, froth, teeth   **(6 marks)**
Challenge 3
1. a) I have four fingers and one <u>thumb</u> on each hand.
    b) I heard a loud <u>thud</u> when the girl jumped off the bed.
    c) I like the story of the <u>three</u> little pigs.
    d) A <u>thief</u> stole the big diamond.
    e) The opposite of fat is <u>thin</u>.
    f) I <u>thank</u> my friend for my present. **(6 marks)**

Pages 26–27
Challenge 1
1. a) but/ton   b) cof/fee   c) hel/met
    d) pic/nic   e) sis/ter   f) fin/ish
    g) lem/on   h) hab/it   i) lad/der
                                              (9 marks)

Challenge 2
1. a) Sun + day   b) chest + nut
    c) bed + room   d) back + pack
                                              (4 marks)
2. a) jelly<u>fish</u>   b) nut<u>shell</u>
    c) pop<u>corn</u>   d) tea<u>pot</u>   **(4 marks)**
Challenge 3
1. a) zeb/ra; 2   b) el/e/phant; 3
    c) pan/da; 2   d) kan/ga/roo; 3
                                              (4 marks)
2. a) robin   b) dragon
    c) thunder   d) kitten   **(4 marks)**

Pages 28–29
Challenge 1
1. a) miss, fuss, hiss, toss, pass
    b) less, moss, dress, kiss, boss   **(10 marks)**
2. a) chill, well, dull, ball, smell
    b) sell, bill, shell, shall, doll **(10 marks)**
Challenge 2
1. a) huff, stiff, puff, cliff, stuff
    b) bluff, chuff, off, cuff, quiff **(10 marks)**
2. buzz, jazz, fizz, whizz, fuzz   **(5 marks)**
3. a) I saw a rocket <u>whizz</u> up into space.
    b) The bees <u>buzz</u> around the flowers.
    c) The man played <u>jazz</u> on his clarinet.
                                              (3 marks)

Challenge 3
1. a) frill, press, cress, thrill, troll
    b) cross, still, chess, spill, spell **(10 marks)**
2. a) My dad was <u>cross</u> when I spilled my milk.
    b) The witch cast a <u>spell</u> on her cat.
    c) The <u>troll</u> ran from the giant.   **(3 marks)**
3. a) better, rabbit, kitten, hobbit
    b) ribbon, attic, bobbin, butter   **(8 marks)**

Answers

Challenge 1
1. moon, roof, boot, spoon, book, tools, hook, soon, wool, wood **(10 marks)**

Challenge 2
1. a) moon, spoon   b) hoop, coop
   c) zoom, boom   d) food, mood
   e) look, hook   f) tool, fool **(12 marks)**
2. seen, teen, week, tree, green, heel, bee, feet, been, feel **(10 marks)**

Challenge 3
1. a) At night, I <u>look</u> up at the <u>moon</u>.
   b) I put my <u>foot</u> into my <u>boot</u>.
   c) The man <u>took</u> some <u>wood</u> and his <u>tools</u> on to the <u>roof</u>.
   d) I eat my <u>food</u> with a <u>spoon</u>.
   e) I am reading a <u>book</u> about Captain <u>Hook</u>.
   f) I sweep the <u>room</u> with a <u>broom</u>. **(6 marks)**
2. a) week, seek   b) keep, peep
   c) feet, meet   d) weed, need
   e) wheel, feel   f) been, seen
   g) three, tree   h) reef, beef
   (8 marks)
3. a) The leaves on the <u>trees</u> are <u>green</u>.
   b) Next <u>week</u>, I will plant some <u>seeds</u> in the garden.
   c) Mum will come along the <u>street</u> and <u>meet</u> me from school. **(6 marks)**

Pages 32–33
Challenge 1
1. a) big, sack, hop
   b) can, cog, kit
   c) tin, well, buzz **(9 marks)**

Challenge 2
1. a) shap, thit, pumt
   b) malk, twop, moch
   c) felk, drap, bleck **(9 marks)**
2. a) My dog loves to <u>bark</u> at cats.
   b) I can play with my <u>toys</u>.
   c) When I visit my <u>gran</u> she gives me cakes.
   d) The <u>ship</u> sailed across the sea.
   e) I like to drink <u>milk</u> at lunch time.
   f) I saw the <u>flag</u> blowing in the wind.
   (6 marks)

Challenge 3
1. da   st
   cli   mp
   fi   ld
   fo   ck **(4 marks)**
2. a) Award 1 mark for each correctly spelled real word made of these letters.

b) Award 1 mark for each made-up word using these letters. **(12 marks)**

Pages 34–35
Challenge 1
1. Award 1 mark for each word learned and written correctly from memory. **(5 marks)**
2. a) It was cold <u>so</u> I put on my coat.
   b) Sam went to feed <u>his</u> rabbit.
   c) What shall we <u>do</u> when we have finished our work?
   d) My friend <u>has</u> a dog.
   e) Mum said there was <u>no</u> time for a story before bed. **(5 marks)**

Challenge 2
1. a) I have <u>one</u> brother and <u>one</u> sister.
   b) My friend came to my <u>house</u> to play.
   c) I am going to <u>ask</u> for a bike for my birthday.
   d) <u>Once</u> upon a time, there lived a magic frog.
   e) We are going on holiday <u>today</u>. **(6 marks)**

Challenge 3
1. Award 1 mark for each word learned and written correctly from memory. **(12 marks)**
2. Award 1 mark for each sentence written using each of the words. **(5 marks)**

Pages 36–37
Challenge 1
1. a) butter, sugar, eggs, flour **(4 marks)**
   b) cake cases **(1 mark)**
   c) wash your hands **(1 mark)**
   d) turn on the oven **(1 mark)**

Challenge 2
1. a) butter and sugar **(2 marks)**
   b) eggs **(1 mark)**
   c) whisk them **(1 mark)**
   d) flour **(1 mark)**

Challenge 3
1. a) Spoon the mixture into <u>cake cases</u>.
   b) Put them into the oven for about <u>20 minutes</u>.
   c) When they are cool you can <u>decorate them</u>. **(3 marks)**
2. So the icing does not melt; so the cakes set properly in the right shape; or any other relevant reason. **(2 marks)**

Pages 38–39
Challenge 1
1. a) riding his bike **(1 mark)**
   b) a buzzing noise **(1 mark)**

c) a big round shape (with red and green flashing lights) **(1 mark)**

d) red and green **(2 marks)**

e) three **(1 mark)**

Challenge 2

1. a) big and round with sticking up spikes

b) it jumped on Jack's bike and rode round the garden

c) it ran to Jack's ball and kicked it over the fence

d) it climbed the ladder and slid down Jack's slide **(4 marks)**

Challenge 3

1. a) Ekib, Llab, Edils **(3 marks)**

b) Bike, Ball, Slide **(3 marks)**

c) 'Yes' or 'no' acceptable **(1 mark)**

d) Award mark for the reason **(1 mark)**

Pages 40–41
Challenge 1

1. a) in forests and mountains **(1 mark)**

b) climbing trees **(1 mark)**

c) **Any three from:** grass, roots, berries, fish, insects, mammals, birds. **(3 marks)**

d) in winter **(1 mark)**

Challenge 2

1. a) white **(1 mark)**

b) in the Arctic **(1 mark)**

c) seals **(1 mark)**

d) **Any two from:** walrus, beluga, birds' eggs. **(2 marks)**

e) about the size of a guinea pig **(1 mark)**

Challenge 3

1. a) true b) false

c) false d) false **(4 marks)**

Pages 42–43
Challenge 1

1. a) a loud noise/nee-nah-nee-nah **(1 mark)**

b) a fire engine **(1 mark)**

c) red, silver, blue **(3 marks)**

d) "I'm going to be a fireman when I grow up" **(1 mark)**

Challenge 2

1. a) Mum, Dad, Tim **(3 marks)**

b) she felt someone pulling her hair **(1 mark)**

c) the monkey waved as if to say, "It was me!" **(1 mark)**

d) "Cheeky monkey!" **(1 mark)**

Challenge 3

1. a) Erin loved the seaside. **(1 mark)**

b) She ran towards the sea with her bucket. **(2 marks)**

c) She collected five shells, six round pebbles and an empty crab shell. **(2 marks)**

d) Together they made a giant sandcastle. **(1 mark)**

Pages 44–45
Challenge 1

1. Award 10 marks for perfect recitation, 8 marks for five lines, 6 marks for four lines, 4 marks for three lines, 2 marks for two lines. **(10 marks)**

Challenge 2

1. a) wide-eyed

b) claws

c) nose

d) twit-twoo **(4 marks)**

2. a) I saw a little fox sitting in a box.

b) I heard a hissing snake. I think its name was Jake.

c) Inside an old dark house, I saw a tiny mouse.

d) I saw an old brown goat riding in a boat. **(4 marks)**

Challenge 3

1. a) a little fox b) a hissing snake

c) a tiny mouse d) a butting goat **(4 marks)**

2. Award 1 mark (up to 2 marks per animal) for each describing word for each animal. **(8 marks)**

Pages 46–49
Progress Test 1

1. a)–f), award 1 mark per answer to the questions. **(6 marks)**

2. a) We sat on the beach at the bottom of the cliff.

b) Amy jumped off the board into the pool.

c) The card was so stiff I could not bend it.

d) Will the wolf huff and puff and blow the house down? **(5 marks)**

3. a) munch, finch, much, beach, cheese

b) chill, such, chick, chair, cheep **(10 marks)**

4. a) bam/boo b) hob/bit c) wag/on

d) top/ic e) car/rot f) but/ter

g) fif/teen h) can/dy i) poc/ket **(9 marks)**

5. a) A zebra is an animal with black and white stripes.

Answers

b) When I go to school I carry my <u>backpack</u> on my back.

c) A baby cat is called a <u>kitten</u>.

d) The man climbed a <u>ladder</u> to clean the windows.

e) The <u>dentist</u> looks after my teeth.

(5 marks)

6. a) false   **b)** false

c) true   **d)** false

e) true   **f)** true   **(6 marks)**

7. a) fox, box

b) cat; **any one word from:** bat, fat, hat, mat, pat, rat, sat, vat or other

c) dog; **any one word from:** bog, cog, fog, hog, jog, log or other

d) pig; **any one word from:** dig, big, fig, gig, jig, rig, wig or other

e) mouse; **any one word from:** house, louse or other

f) goat; **any one word from:** boat, coat, float, moat, note, quote, stoat, vote or other   **(6 marks)**

8. a) I have <u>been</u> to London to visit the <u>queen</u>.

b) My sister and I <u>shoot</u> down the chute at the swimming <u>pool</u>.

c) I have a <u>cheese</u> sandwich for my lunch at <u>school</u>.

d) When I put on my <u>boot</u> I <u>feel</u> a hard stone.   **(8 marks)**

9. a) Mum said I <u>was</u> a very good girl at the shops.

b) I will give <u>you</u> a lovely present.

c) We are going <u>to</u> see my favourite film today.

d) For my party food we will have fish <u>and</u> chips.   **(4 marks)**

Pages 50–51
Challenge 1

1. a) cave, **b)** five, **c)** carve, **d)** live, **e)** have, **f)** shave, **g)** arrive, **h)** love, **i)** save, **j)** hive

(10 marks)

2. a) Bees make honey in a <u>beehive</u>.

b) I can <u>dive</u> into the swimming pool.

c) My mum can <u>drive</u> a big truck.

d) I have <u>twelve</u> friends coming to my party.

(4 marks)

Challenge 2

1.
glove   sleeve
wave   give
arrive   love
leave   dive
live   gave   **(5 marks)**

2. a) batch **b)** pitch **c)** watch **d)** hutch **e)** witch

f) latch **g)** notch **h)** fetch **i)** hatch   **(9 marks)**

Challenge 3

1. a) try, fly, spy, cry, fry, why, shy, by

b) very, merry, fairy, happy, puppy, windy, silly, mummy   **(16 marks)**

2. a) It was <u>windy</u> so we went out to <u>fly</u> a kite.

b) The <u>silly</u> clown made us laugh.

c) My <u>mummy</u> takes me to school every day.

(3 marks)

Pages 52–53
Challenge 1

1. a) light, tight, fight, might, fright, sight, sigh

b) side, bite, like, kite   **(11 marks)**

Challenge 2

1. a) The loud noise gave me a <u>fright</u>.

b) <u>My</u> sister upset me and made me <u>cry</u>.

c) I can <u>tie</u> <u>my</u> shoelaces.

d) A button popped off because my coat was too <u>tight</u>.

e) I <u>like</u> to play in the park.

f) I use my teeth to <u>bite</u> my food. **(8 marks)**

2. Any three words with i_e, e.g. line, tribe etc.

(3 marks)

3. a) Any two from: boy, coy, joy, soy or others.

b) Any two from: foil, soil, toil or others.

c) Any two from: coin, join or others.

(6 marks)

Challenge 3

1. a) I found my lost tractor in the <u>toy</u> box.

b) I am a <u>boy</u> and my sister is a girl.

c) I tossed a <u>coin</u> into the fountain and made a wish.   **(3 marks)**

2. a) train, chain, brain ✓
take, name, shade

b) Any three from: bay, clay, day, gay, hay, jay, lay, may, pay, play, pray, ray, say, stay, stray, tray, way or others.   **(9 marks)**

Pages 54–55
Challenge 1

1. Award 1 mark per day spelled correctly in good handwriting with capital letter. **(7 marks)**

2. a) 7   **(1 mark)**

b) Saturday and Sunday   **(2 marks)**

Challenge 2

1. a) Tuesday   **(1 mark)**

b) Sunday, Monday, Friday   **(3 marks)**

c) Wednesday   **(1 mark)**

Challenge 3

1. a)–g) Award 1 mark for each finished sentence beginning with the days of the week.

(7 marks)

2. **a)–g)** Award 1 mark for each day spelled correctly from memory. **(7 marks)**

Pages 56–57
Challenge 1
1. **a)** longer   **b)** smaller
   c) cheaper   **d)** cleaner
   e) kinder   **(5 marks)**
2. **a)** Alex is <u>taller</u> than Sam.
   b) Sam is <u>shorter</u> than Alex. **(2 marks)**

Challenge 2
1. **a)** strongest   **b)** meanest
   c) thickest   **d)** lightest
   e) darkest   **(5 marks)**
2. **a)** The horse wanted to eat the <u>greenest</u> grass.
   b) My mum bought the <u>cheapest</u> pair of shoes in the shop.
   c) At night, the sky is the <u>darkest</u> shade of blue. **(3 marks)**

Challenge 3
1. **a)** colder, coldest
   b) louder, loudest
   c) quicker, quickest   **(6 marks)**
2. **a)** The fridge is <u>colder</u> than the kitchen, but the freezer is the <u>coldest</u>.
   b) I can shout <u>louder</u> than you, but my brother is the <u>loudest</u>.
   c) When we raced, Helen was <u>quicker</u> than Tom, but I was the <u>quickest</u>. **(6 marks)**

Pages 58–59
Challenge 1
1. **a)** fern, kerb, verb
   b) term, her, perch
   c) herd, germ, hers   **(9 marks)**
2. **a)** The little girl played with <u>her</u> doll.
   b) We start a new <u>term</u> after the holidays.
   c) There is a <u>herd</u> of cows in the field.
   d) A <u>verb</u> is a doing or being word.
   e) I stand on the <u>kerb</u> and look both ways before I cross the road. **(5 marks)**

Challenge 2
1. Any three words with ir, for example:
   girl, bird, dirt   **(3 marks)**
2. Any three words with ur, for example:
   turn, burn, hurt   **(3 marks)**
3. **a)** I got my hands <u>dirty</u> in the garden.
   b) The <u>bird</u> was sitting on its nest.
   c) I saw a <u>girl</u> running away from me.
   d) I <u>stir</u> some milk into my tea. **(4 marks)**

Challenge 3
1. **a)** <u>bone</u>, <u>joke</u>
   boat, soap, toast
   b) <u>robe</u>, <u>nose</u>, <u>doze</u>
   load, toad
   c) <u>zone</u>, <u>rope</u>
   croak, road, loaf   **(15 marks)**
2. **a)** I use <u>soap</u> to wash my hands.
   b) I heard a <u>toad</u> <u>croak</u> down by the pond.
   c) Dad cuts the <u>loaf</u> of bread to make some <u>toast</u>.
   d) The clown had a red <u>nose</u>. He told a funny <u>joke</u>. **(7 marks)**

Pages 60–61
Challenge 1
1. **a)** I was too <u>slow</u> so I missed the bus.
   b) When I <u>grow</u> up I will be an athlete.
   c) I hid <u>below</u> the bridge so no one could find me.
   d) I watched the river <u>flow</u> past me.
   e) The field was covered in white <u>snow</u>.
                            (5 marks)

Challenge 2
1. **a)** **One word from:** crown, frown, town or other correct word.
   b) **One word from:** prowl, howl or other correct word.
   c) **One word from:** flower, cower, power, bower or other correct word. **(3 marks)**

Challenge 3
1. **a)** **One word from:** around, sound, found, pound or other correct word.
   b) south
   c) loud
   d) **One word from:** out, about, pout or other correct word. **(4 marks)**
2. Inside the cow: crown, town, shower, clown, flower, cow, frown.
   Inside the mouth: around, hound, proud, mouth, about, loud, pout, found, round.
                          (16 marks)

Pages 62–63
Challenge 1
1. phonics, alphabet, phone   **(3 marks)**
2. elephant, dolphin   **(2 marks)**
3. Rudolph, Sophie, Phuong   **(3 marks)**

Challenge 2
1. **a)** I saw an <u>elephant</u> at the zoo.
   b) I like to sing <u>Rudolph</u> the Red-nosed Reindeer.
   c) I know all the letters of the <u>alphabet</u>.
   d) The <u>dolphin</u> swims quickly and jumps out of the water. **(4 marks)**

Answers

2. a) The <u>white</u> cat had long <u>whiskers</u>.
   b) The old cart has lost a <u>wheel</u>.
   c) I heard a <u>whistle</u> then a quiet <u>whisper</u>.
   (5 marks)

3. a) <u>When</u> can you come to my house to play?
   b) <u>Why</u> did you run away?
   c) <u>What</u> would you like for tea?
   d) <u>Which</u> cake would you like?
   e) <u>Where</u> shall we go tomorrow?   **(5 marks)**

Challenge 3
1. a) A baby <u>kangaroo</u> is called a joey.
   b) Dad boiled the <u>kettle</u> to make a cup of tea.
   c) A <u>kitten</u> is a baby cat.
   d) A <u>koala</u> is an Australian animal.   **(4 marks)**
2. a) king   **b)** kite
   c) kit   **d)** kid   **(4 marks)**

Pages 64–65
Challenge 1
1. star — lark
   dart — car
   mark — tart   **(3 marks)**

Challenge 2
1. a) smart   **b)** shark
   c) bark   **d)** start   **(4 marks)**
2. a) I eat my dinner with a knife and <u>fork</u>.
   b) I switched on my <u>torch</u> when the lights went out.
   c) The boy blew loudly on his toy <u>horn</u>.
   d) The ship sailed into <u>port</u>.   **(4 marks)**

Challenge 3
1. In any order a)–e): storm, form; port, fort; horn, corn; cord, ford; porch, torch. **(10 marks)**

Pages 66–67
Challenge 1
1. a) grit, frog, drip, clap
   b) stop, skin, flat
   c) swim, scab, plan   **(10 marks)**
2. drab — twin
   stop — drip
   slip — slap
   skin — crab
   clap — plop   **(5 marks)**

Challenge 2
1. a) lost, desk, bank
   b) left, land, junk
   c) wasp, lift, gulp, risk   **(10 marks)**
2. a) best, rest   **b)** camp, lamp
   c) loft, soft   **d)** must, just

e) melt, belt   **f)** pump, bump
g) land, hand   **h)** bent, went
   (8 marks)

Challenge 3
1. a) track **c)** twist **d)** crank **f)** crisp **g)** trunk
   j) stamp   **(6 marks)**
2. a)–d) Award 1 mark for each sentence that includes the word.   **(4 marks)**

Pages 68–71
Progress Test 2
1. a) Any three words from: drain, grain, gain, lain, plain, rain, stain, Spain, slain, train or others.
   b) Any three words from: came, blame, dame, fame, flame, frame, game, lame, name, tame or others.
   c) Any three words from: bay, clay, day, dray, fray, gay, hay, jay, lay, may, pay, play, pray, ray, say, stay, sway, way or others.
   (9 marks)
2. Monday, Tuesday, Wednesday, Thursday, Friday   **(5 marks)**
3. a) A palace is <u>grander</u> than a house.
   b) A feather is <u>lighter</u> than a stone.
   c) A snake is <u>longer</u> than a worm.
   d) A cheetah is <u>quicker</u> than an elephant.
   e) A trumpet is <u>louder</u> than a whisper.
   (5 marks)

4.

Words that rhyme with try	Words with a y ending that sound like ee
by	mummy
cry	puppy
my	sloppy
buy	sunny
sty	happy
why	sorry

(12 marks)

5. week, meet, jeep, green, see, sheep, creep, feed, feet, asleep   **(10 marks)**
6. a) I fell over and <u>hurt</u> my knee.
   b) It is my <u>turn</u> to play on the swing.
   c) Dad put a log on the fire to <u>burn</u>.
   (3 marks)
7. a) cheese   **b)** coach
   c) cheek   **d)** chin
   e) chicken   **f)** much   **(6 marks)**
8. a) puppy   **b)** bedroom
   c) picnic   **d)** sixteen
   e) ladder   **(5 marks)**

Pages 72–73
Challenge 1
1. a) Award 1 mark for 'Once upon a time'.
(1 mark)
   b) Award 1, 2 or 3 marks depending on the amount of detail in the answer. **(3 marks)**
Challenge 2
1. a) yes or no acceptable **(1 mark)**
   b) Award 1, 2 or 3 marks depending on the amount of detail in the answer. **(3 marks)**
Challenge 3
1. a) yes or no acceptable **(1 mark)**
   b) Award 1 mark for an idea. **(1 mark)**

Pages 74–75
Challenge 1
1. a) Award 2 marks for story, with up to 2 marks given for greater detail. **(4 marks)**
   b) Award 1 mark for a location given.
(1 mark)
2. a) Award 1 mark for name of main character.
(1 mark)
   b) Award 1 mark for each name of two other characters. **(2 marks)**
3. Award 1 mark for a characteristic. **(1 mark)**
Challenge 2
1. Award a maximum of 2 marks for each box (1–6). **(12 marks)**
2. Award 1 mark for talking about sentence and 1 mark for writing. **(2 marks)**
Challenge 3
1. Award 1 mark for talking about sequence and 1 mark for writing. **(2 marks)**
2. Award 2 marks for talking about sequence and 3 marks for writing. **(5 marks)**
3. Award 1 mark for talking about the ending and 1 mark for writing it. **(2 marks)**

Pages 76–77
Challenge 1
1. Correct order:
   1. b) A bird made a nest.
   2. c) Then the bird laid five eggs.
   3. a) Five chicks hatched out of the eggs.
(3 marks)
2. 1 mark for one answer, e.g. The bird fed the chicks; The baby birds flew away. **(1 mark)**
Challenge 2
1. Correct order:
   1. d) Take two slices of bread.
   2. b) Spread the bread with butter.
   3. e) Cut slices of cheese.
   4. a) Put the cheese on one slice of bread.

5. c) Put the second slice of bread on top of the first one. **(5 marks)**
2. Any proper sentence. **(1 mark)**
Challenge 3
1. Correct order:
   1. d) We got to the seaside at 10 o'clock.
   2. f) The first thing we did was make a big sandcastle.
   3. e) Then we ran to the sea to wash off the sand.
   4. b) After that, we had our picnic lunch.
   5. c) In the afternoon, we swam in the sea.
   6. a) It was time to go home so we went back to the car. **(6 marks)**
2. Sentences written out in the same order as **1.**, above. **(6 marks)**

Pages 78–79
Challenge 1
1. Award 1 mark for each of a)–d). **(4 marks)**
Challenge 2
1. Award 1 mark for each of 1, 2, 3, 4, 5.
(5 marks)
2. Award 1 or 2 marks depending on the amount of detail in the answer. **(2 marks)**
Challenge 3
1. Award 1 mark for each part of the story, 1–7. Award up to 3 marks extra for handwriting, spacing, spelling and punctuation used.
(10 marks)

Pages 80–81
Challenge 1
1. Award 1 mark for each part of letter a)–c).
(3 marks)
Challenge 2
1. Award 1 mark for each part of letter a)–d).
(4 marks)
Challenge 3
1. Award 1 mark for each part of letter a)–d). Award up to 3 marks extra for handwriting, spacing, spelling and punctuation used.
(7 marks)

Pages 82–83
Challenge 1
1. Award 1 mark for talking about the programme and 1 mark for writing. **(2 marks)**
2. 1 mark per answer. **(3 marks)**
Challenge 2
1. Award 1 mark per sentence about the park, up to a total of 5 marks. **(5 marks)**
2. 1 mark for answer. **(1 mark)**

Answers

Challenge 3

1. Award 1 mark per sentence about the outing, up to a total of 5 marks. **(5 marks)**
2. 1 mark per answer for **a)–c)**. **(3 marks)**

Pages 84–87
Progress Test 3

1. a) false   b) false
    c) true   d) false
    e) true   f) true   **(6 marks)**
2. a) My grandad <u>said</u> he was coming to dinner.
    b) I do not know <u>where</u> I left my coat.
    c) My friends told me <u>they</u> would meet me at school.
    d) How <u>are</u> you?   **(4 marks)**
3. a) The <u>greedy</u> boy ate all the cakes.
    b) The lights were <u>bright</u> and <u>sparkling</u> on the tree.
    c) Henry was rescued by a <u>brave</u> person.
    d) I have a <u>fantastic</u> collection of cars.
    e) I have a <u>lumpy</u> pillow on my bed. **(6 marks)**
4. a) shorter, shortest
    b) brighter, brightest
    c) slower, slowest   **(6 marks)**
5. match, latch, patch, catch, thatch, hatch **(6 marks)**
6. a) elephant   b) e.g. Sophie
    c) dolphin   d) phonics
    e) alphabet   **(5 marks)**
7. a) **Any word from:** brave, cave, Dave, gave, grave, nave, knave, rave, save, stave, wave or other.
    b) **Any word from:** above, dove, love or other. **(2 marks)**
8. a) white   **(1 mark)**
    b) black crosses   **(1 mark)**
    c) red   **(1 mark)**
    d) floppy and yellow   **(2 marks)**
    e) green and red   **(2 marks)**
    f) baggy   **(1 mark)**
    g) Award marks for the correct details and colours used.   **(2 marks)**

Pages 88–89
Challenge 1

1.
book	books	tin	tins
brick	bricks	ship	ships
ant	ants	light	lights
cup	cups	peg	pegs
		rug	rugs

(9 marks)

Challenge 2

1.
fizz	fizzes	arch	arches
peach	peaches	bus	buses
boss	bosses	dress	dresses
hutch	hutches	ditch	ditches
six	sixes	fox	foxes
		smash	smashes

(11 marks)

Challenge 3

1.
buzz	buzzes	kiss	kisses
elephant	elephants	banana	bananas
melon	melons	box	boxes
witch	witches	gas	gases
hill	hills	name	names
crash	crashes	tax	taxes

(12 marks)

2. a) The third little pig's house was made of <u>bricks</u>.
    b) The monkey ate six <u>bananas</u> and threw the skins on the ground.
    c) At home, I have three <u>boxes</u> full of toys.
    d) The children stood in a row and told me their <u>names</u>.   **(4 marks)**

Pages 90–91
Challenge 1

1. a) <u>fish and chips</u> written with finger spaces
    b) <u>brother and sister</u> written with finger spaces
    c) <u>in the park</u> written with finger spaces **(3 marks)**

Challenge 2

1. a) i or I acceptable as capital has not been asked for
    b) i or I acceptable as capital has not been asked for
    c) we or We acceptable as capital has not been asked for   **(3 marks)**

Challenge 3

1. a) Sentence written clearly beginning with a capital letter and ending with a full stop.
    b) Sentence written clearly beginning with a capital letter and ending with a full stop.
    c) Sentence written clearly beginning with a capital letter and ending with a full stop. **(3 marks)**

2. a) Sentence written clearly beginning with a capital letter and ending with a full stop.
    b) Sentence written clearly beginning with a capital letter and ending with a full stop.
    c) Sentence written clearly beginning with a capital letter and ending with a full stop.
    d) Sentence written clearly beginning with a capital letter and ending with a full stop.
                                        (4 marks)

Pages 92–93
Challenge 1
1. a) Circle t at beginning and after chair.
    b) Circle t at beginning and after teeth.
    c) Circle t at beginning and after bow.
    d) Circle t at beginning and after nose.
    e) Circle t at beginning and after nine.
                                        (10 marks)
Challenge 2
    a) Sentence written clearly with capital I and full stop at the end.
    b) Sentence written clearly with capital I and full stop at the end.
    c) Sentence written clearly with capital T and full stop at the end.
    d) Sentence written clearly with capital T and full stop at the end.
    e) Sentence written clearly with capital T and full stop at the end.   **(10 marks)**
Challenge 3
1. a) I like to eat an apple for lunch. Apples are sweet and juicy.
    b) The dog ran across the grass. It ran after a cat.
    c) The elephant has white tusks. They are quite long.
    d) The plane landed at the airport. The people had been on holiday.   **(8 marks)**

Pages 94–95
Challenge 1
1. a) In winter, I put on my gloves so I can go outside.
    b) I love going to the fair because I love the rides.
    c) My brother is taller than me because I am much younger.
    d) I think a cat is the best animal and I love to hear it purr.   **(9 marks)**

Challenge 2
1. a) I invited Rose, Sandeep, Erin and David to my party.
    b) My sister Esha said I was silly.
    c) Yash and Grace played with the cars, but I played by myself.
    d) Narinda and I went up and down on the seesaw.
    e) My teacher is called Mrs West and I like her.
    f) I think I will beat Amy in the race because I can run fast.   **(21 marks)**
Challenge 3
1. a) Yesterday, I went to London.
    b) Paris is the capital of France.
    c) Sami and I went to Brighton, which is by the sea.
    d) We went to Spain on holiday and I went to the beach.   **(11 marks)**

Pages 96–97
Challenge 1
1. a) Where are you going?
    b) Why do you want to come to the fair?
    c) Do you like pizza or salad best?
    d) When will you get a pet?
    e) What is your favourite animal?   **(5 marks)**
2. a) Do you like horses? Yes or no.
    b) Would you like to ride a horse? Yes or no.   **(2 marks)**
Challenge 2
1. a) What is a baby dog called? a puppy
    b) What is a baby cat called? a kitten
    c) What is a baby sheep called? a lamb
    d) What is a baby pig called? a piglet
    e) What is a baby fox called? a cub
    f) What is a baby chicken called? a chick   **(6 marks)**
2. a) My dad reads to me at bedtime.
    b) Does your mum have long hair?
    c) When will you come and play with me?
    d) The baby is very happy.   **(4 marks)**
Challenge 3
1. a) Award 1 mark for a suitable question.
    b) Award 1 mark for a suitable question.
    c) Award 2 marks, 1 mark for each speech bubble.   **(4 marks)**

Pages 98–99
Challenge 1
1. a) Look out!
    b) How exciting!

Answers

c) What a lucky girl you are!
d) That is a lovely big parcel!
e) Wow! **(5 marks)**

Challenge 2
1. a) I cannot believe it!
   b) You have grown such a lot since April!
   c) Be quiet!
   d) What a lot of books you have read!
   e) How fantastic! **(5 marks)**
2. a) Mum and I went to the shops.
   b) The hat she bought was fabulous!
   c) It was amazing!
   d) We came home and showed Dad.
   e) Dad said it was fantastic! **(5 marks)**

Challenge 3
1. a) We went to the zoo on Saturday.
   b) What did you see there?
   c) We saw an elephant.
   d) Was it big?
   e) It was enormous! **(5 marks)**
2. a) I have been out with my gran.
   b) Where did you go?
   c) She took me to see a film.
   d) Did you have a good time? **(4 marks)**
3. Made-up answer in a sentence, with correct punctuation. **(1 mark)**

Pages 100–101
Challenge 1
1. a) fish and chips   b) shoes and socks
   c) bucket and spade d) horse and cart
   e) cup and saucer   f) knife and fork
   g) bacon and eggs   h) left and right
   i) king and queen   j) boys and girls
   (10 marks)

Challenge 2
1. a) dark and light   b) hard and soft/easy
   c) big and small/little d) happy and sad
   e) heavy and light   f) empty and full
   g) hot and cold   h) fast and slow
   (8 marks)
2. a) I am a boy and my name is Jack.
   b) I can run fast and I win all the races.
   c) I love reading and I have lots of books.
   d) I have a cat and her name is Tabby.
   e) I play with Ling and she is my best friend.
   (5 marks)

Challenge 3
1. a)–d) 1 mark for each sentence with and and an ending. **(4 marks)**
2. a) My brother is called Ethan and my sister is called Emily.
   b) I like apples and bananas, but my favourite fruits are strawberries and cherries. **(2 marks)**

Pages 102–103
Challenge 1
1. a) unhappy   b) undo
   c) unfit   d) unlucky
   e) unpack   **(5 marks)**

Challenge 2
1. a) untie   b) undress
   c) untidy   d) uneven
   e) untrue   **(5 marks)**
2. a) unhook   b) untidy
   c) untrue   d) unplug
   e) unload   **(5 marks)**

Challenge 3
1. a) I helped Dad unload the dishwasher.
   b) Your buttons are undone.
   c) Help me unzip my coat.
   d) The padlock needs a key to unlock it.
   e) I am feeling a bit unwell. **(5 marks)**
2. a) unhappy   b) unwell
   c) undress   d) unsafe **(4 marks)**

Pages 104–105
Challenge 1
1. a) helping   b) jumping
   c) following   d) climbing
   e) opening   f) kicking **(6 marks)**

Challenge 2
1. a) helped   b) jumped
   c) followed   d) climbed
   e) opened   f) kicked **(6 marks)**
2. a) Mum opened the window to let the fresh air in.
   b) I climbed a mountain when we were on holiday.
   c) I jumped up and down on the trampoline.
   (3 marks)

Challenge 3
1. a) helper   b) jumper
   c) follower   d) climber
   e) opener   f) kicker **(6 marks)**

2. a) The dog <u>followed</u> the man all the way home.
    b) I love being a <u>helper</u> in the classroom.
    c) A sheep looks like it is wearing a woolly <u>jumper</u>!
    d) Dad was <u>opening</u> a tin of dog food with a tin <u>opener</u>. **(5 marks)**

Pages 106–107
Challenge 1
1. Award 1 mark for each of **a)–f)** provided the child gives answers that meet the requirements for a story. **(6 marks)**
2. Award 2 marks for how the characters begin the story; 2 marks for each of three stages of the story; 2 marks for the ending. Spelling, grammar and punctuation are not an issue at this stage. **(10 marks)**

Challenge 2
1. Award up to 5 marks for correction of spelling, especially if the spelling mistake is spotted by the child. **(5 marks)**
2. Award up to 5 marks for correction of punctuation, especially if the mistake is spotted by the child. **(5 marks)**

Challenge 3
1. Award up to 10 marks for neat handwriting, correct spellings and punctuation in the rewrite. **(10 marks)**
2. Award up to 5 marks for child checking the story and reading it out loud. **(5 marks)**

Pages 108–112
Progress Test 4
1. a) <u>J</u>ack and <u>M</u>ia went to <u>L</u>ondon.
    b) <u>I</u> have a best friend called <u>P</u>ippa.
    c) <u>I</u> go to school on <u>M</u>onday, <u>T</u>uesday, <u>W</u>ednesday, <u>T</u>hursday and <u>F</u>riday. **(3 marks)**
2. a) ship   b) shell
    c) shop   d) shut
    e) shack   **(5 marks)**
3. a) buses   b) watches
    c) legs   d) stairs
    e) patches   f) boys
    g) laptops   h) hisses
    i) flashes   **(9 marks)**

4. d) Little Red Riding Hood waved goodbye to her mum.
    b) First she picked some flowers in the woods.
    a) Then she went to her grandmother's house.
    e) A wolf was in her grandmother's bed.
    f) The wolf had eaten Little Red Riding Hood's grandmother.
    c) A woodcutter rescued Little Red Riding Hood. **(12 marks)**
5. a) <u>When</u> would you like to go to the beach?
    b) <u>Which</u> teddy bear would you like?
    c) <u>Why</u> are you crying?
    d) <u>What</u> is the time?
    e) <u>Where</u> did you put my pencil? **(5 marks)**
6. a) **Any two from:** loud, proud, bowed, crowd, vowed.
    b) **Any two from:** brown, clown, crown, frown, gown, town or others.
    c) **Any two from:** how, cow, sow, row, wow, bow or others.
    d) **Any two from:** around, sound, hound, mound, found, pound, round or others. **(8 marks)**
7. Award 1 mark for each **a)–d)** if word is spelled correctly from memory. **(4 marks)**
8. a) I always <u>put</u> my toys away when I have finished playing.
    b) Will you <u>come</u> to my house for tea?
    c) I tried to <u>pull</u> open the door but it was locked.
    d) I have <u>some</u> pencils in a box. **(4 marks)**
9. a) What a noise they are making<u>!</u>
    b) Would you like a slice of melon<u>?</u>
    c) I love seeing spring flowers in the woods<u>.</u>
    d) The ostrich is a very large bird, but it cannot fly<u>.</u>
    e) How marvellous you look<u>!</u>
    f) How old are you<u>?</u> **(6 marks)**
10. a) mi<u>lk</u>   b) cri<u>sp</u> or cri<u>mp</u>
    c) chi<u>mp</u>   d) be<u>nd</u>
    e) plu<u>mp</u>   f) da<u>mp</u>
    g) fu<u>nd</u>   h) si<u>lk</u>   **(8 marks)**
11. a) The fish were swimming in a glass <u>tank</u>.
    b) The stone <u>sank</u> to the bottom of the pond.
    c) I love to sleep on the top <u>bunk</u>.
    d) Mum says my bedroom is full of <u>junk</u>. **(4 marks)**

Progress Test Charts

Progress Test 1

Q	Topic	✓ or ✗	See Page
1	Talk about games you like to play		16
2	Double ff		28
3	Add ch		24
4	Split words into syllables		26
5	Two-syllable words		26
6	Answering questions, non-fiction		36
7	Rhyming words		44
8	Double vowels		30
9	Words you know		34

Progress Test 2

Q	Topic	✓ or ✗	See Page
1	Different spellings for sounds		52
2	Days of the week		54
3	Add er to words		56
4	Word endings		50
5	Double vowels		30
6	ur words		58
7	ch words crossword		24
8	Two-syllable words		26

Progress Test Charts

Progress Test 3

Q	Topic	✓ or ✗	See Page
1	True or false non-fiction comprehension		36
2	Words that you know		34
3	Describing words		45
4	Making more and the most: er and est		56
5	Rhyming words		44
6	Words containing ph crossword		62
7	Words ending ve		50
8	Answering questions non-fiction		36

Progress Test 4

Q	Topic	✓ or ✗	See Page
1	Capital letters		92, 94
2	Words beginning with sh		24
3	Making singular words plural		88
4	Putting sentences in the right order		76
5	Questions beginning with wh words		62
6	Rhyming words for ou and ow words		60
7	Words that you know		34
8	Using words in sentences		90
9	Full stops, question marks, exclamation marks		92, 96, 98
10	Word endings		50
11	Words ending nk		22

What am I doing well in? _____

_____

What do I need to improve? _____

_____